Praise for *Opening Doors to Ambitious Primary English*

A treasure trove of ideas for time-impoverished teachers. With the turn of every page, I discovered fresh new inspiration that provides endless possibilities. It is refreshing as the book does not dictate one right way of teaching; rather, it empowers teachers to discover the joy and delight of texts and encourages them to take pupils on this same journey!

Claire Martin-O'Donoghue, Senior Education Leader (East), Diocese of Chichester Academy Trust

Enjoyment of reading is a lifetime gift, and this book will enable you to light the spark leading to growing skills, confidence, enthusiasm and achievement in all aspects of English, even in the most reluctant learner. As important, this book will take you, the professional, on a journey which will reinvigorate your passion for exploring new texts, authors and teaching approaches in the classroom. I thoroughly recommend it.

Denise Yates, author of *Parenting Dual Exceptional Children: Supporting a Child who has High Learning Potential and Special Educational Needs and Disabilities*

This book is informative and exciting, and it contains everything a teacher needs to deliver high-quality English lessons. It opens the door to a deep world of wonder and beauty and provides a myriad of opportunities for imaginative thinking and poetic expression.

Emma Adcock, Principal Teaching and Learning Consultant, VNET Education CIC

The Old English word for 'open' is 'openian', originally meaning 'to reveal' or 'to become manifest'. Revelations are voiced with expertise and awareness in the newest addition to the 'Opening Doors' series – *Opening Doors to Ambitious Primary English*. This new resource for primary educators offers an opportunity to enroot an ardent approach to the teaching of the English curriculum, ensuring challenge for all. Indeed, this evincing work by Bob Cox and co. offers case studies of primary practice alongside innovative ideas for practical classroom application – an opportunity to set actions into motion, ensuring ambitious teaching and learning of English in the primary setting.

Kelly Ashley, education consultant, author of *Word Power: Amplifying Vocabulary Instruction*

This book provides considerable challenge for both teachers and children but, equally, every support to meet that challenge. It has the potential to transform primary English teaching for the better, and in conjunction with the other key approaches mentioned, open doors for children, not only to a more rewarding educational experience, but to richer lives. No primary school should be without it, and many would benefit considerably from associated professional development.

Gordon Askew, MBE, former DfE Reading Adviser, Founder and Chair, English Hubs Council

Another thoroughly researched book from the inimitable Bob Cox, full of exciting suggestions and resources and supported by excellent classroom examples. The collaboration of experts who have worked with Bob to put this text together have drawn upon their own experience to provide an abundance of ideas which teachers cannot fail to be enthused by.

Janet Gough, Primary English Consultant, former NATE Primary Officer

This fantastic book clearly describes how simple and easy-to-replicate strategies such as 'link reading' and 'taster drafts' can be used to engage all pupils using even the most challenging texts with high impact. Lots of real examples of using this toolkit successfully in schools provide teachers with practical tips as well as inspiring ideas demonstrating how by removing the ceiling for our students, possibilities are endless.

Juliet Skellett, School Improvement Advisor, Royal Borough of Greenwich

As a teacher, I have heard high expectations talked about so many times, but what these look like and how to ensure that children are equipped to meet them are not always made clear. Throughout this book, high expectations are mentioned again and again and my feeling, as a reader and a teacher, was that Bob had the same ambitions for me that I have for the learners in my class. I felt challenged as I read this book, but I found that doors truly were opened and that I was given the skills and knowledge needed to truly enable my children to soar. If, like me, you are passionate about honing the craft of teaching, then this book is for you. Teach English as you never have before.

Toria Bono, primary teacher, author of *Tiny Voices Talk*, host of 'Tiny Voice Talks' podcast

Opening Doors to Ambitious Primary English does exactly what it says on the tin. Bob Cox, Leah Crawford, Angela Jenkins and Julie Sargent are relentless in their ambition for all pupils to have access to high-quality texts that become part of their everyday reading and writing diet. The passion and the knowledge of the writers sing from the pages in a way that is inspiring and enthusing but also practical and logical with ideas and strategies to take straight into the classroom. The examples of practice were pertinent and the viewpoints of teaching staff alongside the resulting writing of their pupils shows what can be achieved when we remove the glass ceilings in primary classrooms.

Nicola Mansfield, Primary Curriculum Manager, PiXL

Inspiring accounts from classrooms across the country whose teachers use challenging texts, and apply the principles of Opening Doors, will reignite your passion for teaching and prompt you to reconsider the depth and breadth of texts and the very nature of reading. Practical ways forward abound to enrich the teaching and learning of English, so read, explore, apply and set the bar high for *all* your pupils. This is not an exclusive curriculum, far from it; it is a thoroughly inclusive one which involves teaching to the top.

Professor Teresa Cremin, The Open University

With the renewed focus on reading in schools, there has never been a better time to join the Opening Doors journey. For years, Bob Cox and his team have been working on the promotion of high-quality reading texts in the primary and secondary classroom and how, in turn, that reading can support, develop and improve other areas of the school's curriculum. *Opening Doors to Ambitious Primary English* pulls together the team's wide breadth of research, practice, experience and knowledge of literature into one easy-to-follow and accessible book.

Chris Curtis, English Teacher, Head of English

It is so powerful reading first-hand the experiences teachers and leaders have had in their own school setting. This breaks down the stigma and fear of using 'challenging texts' and makes this accessible and achievable for all teachers, and all leaders nationwide. These case studies pave the way for better English being taught, where challenge is key, because 'challenge' therefore becomes the beating heart of our English curriculum.

Sara Abbas, Year 2 teacher, English Leader, Mulgrave Primary School

This fantastic addition to the 'Opening Doors' series clearly models how schools can design their English curriculum by putting rich, quality texts at the heart. With an emphasis on high challenge, whilst offering strategies that ensure each text can be accessed by all, the reader is offered a toolkit of techniques to inspire exciting and diverse reading and writing responses. These principles are then exemplified in case studies – written by teachers at the chalk face – that are included at the end of each chapter.

Wenda Davies, Languages, Literacy and Communication Lead, Coastlands School

Reading *Opening Doors to Ambitious Primary English* provides further consolidation and real exemplification of the content of the five previous books in the series. The key principles and strategies are expertly explained and the case studies to illustrate each element are invaluable: too often, pedagogical texts provide the 'what' but not always the 'how' and all practitioners, whether they have already embarked upon an Opening Doors journey or have yet to do so, cannot fail to be excited and inspired by the ambition and genuine passion shared by every contributor.

Laura McGeachie, English Lead, Icknield Primary School

As head teacher of an inner-city school with an incredibly diverse community – twenty-four languages spoken – I was determined to be ambitious and not to dumb down our curriculum. The real, practical and adaptable examples in this book are invaluable. The use of challenging, complex texts has ignited passions, stretching and engaging pupils to read more, question more and experience more.

Sam Collier, Head Teacher, Christ Church Upper Armley Church of England Primary School

Opening Doors to Ambitious Primary English is the key to unlock the complete potential of the 'Opening Doors' collection of work – each chapter is laced with the intricacies of all the previous 'Opening Doors' books, and embellished with further examples of practice, research and knowledge, showcasing the stunning potential that many children across the country have achieved. This book empowers educators to exercise equity in every sense of the word, from enabling dialogic talk to deepen children's capacity to make meaning from rich texts, widen vocabulary, cultivate conceptual knowledge and reading links to crafting pieces of writing that rival the greats!

Kiran Satti, Assistant Principal, Primary Trust Literacy Lead Practitioner

OPENING DOORS
to
AMBITIOUS
PRIMARY ENGLISH

Pitching high and including all

Bob Cox

with Leah Crawford, Angela Jenkins and Julie Sargent

Crown House Publishing Limited

www.crownhouse.co.uk

First published by

Crown House Publishing Ltd
Crown Buildings, Bancyfelin, Carmarthen, Wales, SA33 5ND, UK
www.crownhouse.co.uk

and

Crown House Publishing Company LLC
PO Box 2223, Williston, VT 05495, USA
www.crownhousepublishing.com

British Library Cataloguing-in-Publication Data
A catalogue entry for this book is available from the British Library.

Print ISBN 978-178583667-1
Mobi ISBN 978-178583672-5
ePub ISBN 978-178583673-2
ePDF ISBN 978-178583674-9

LCCN 2022948386

Printed and bound in the UK by
Gomer Press, Llandysul, Ceredigion

For all the primary teachers making a difference today and
for the memory of my own at what was then Fetcham
County School in Surrey.

Foreword by Mary Myatt

We are a challenge-seeking species! We like doing things that are difficult, as long as the conditions are characterised by high challenge and low threat.

This is reflected in my conversations with pupils in schools: they enjoy doing work that stretches them. Their observations about the level of challenge they are given can be summarised as 'We'd like more demanding work please!'

I believe there is a tendency in the sector to make things too easy for too many of our pupils, whatever their prior attainment, in the mistaken belief that they can't cope. They can!

In '"Just Reading": The Impact of a Faster Pace of Reading Narratives on the Comprehension of Poorer Adolescent Readers in English Classrooms', Westbrook et al. (2019) from the University of Sussex found that simply reading challenging, complex novels aloud and at a fast pace in each lesson repositioned 'poorer readers' as 'good' readers, giving them a more engaged uninterrupted reading experience over a sustained period.

Feedback from some of the teachers expressed surprise at the impressive results of the poorer readers as they had thought that these pupils would not be able to cope with demanding texts: 'I didn't for a minute expect that they would keep up.'

This research chimes with what the 'Opening Doors' series does, which is to walk us through the steps to create lesson structures in which we can honestly say that every single pupil is immersed in rich and diverse literature and language.

When we're shifting a gear to offer greater challenge to our classes, it's not just the materials we offer but also the rationale for doing so that matters. Change in professional practice will not be embedded until we as teachers understand the 'why' as much as the 'what'. And this is exactly what this marvellous book does.

It's also important that we as professionals up our game in terms of our professional and personal reading. It is through the systems and structures of professional learning within schools that this work needs to be embedded. All the examples of schools working with the Opening Doors materials show not just impressive results and pupils joyful in their reading, but also an excitement amongst staff for this work, which has been supported and encouraged by senior leaders.

Such work rarely takes off on its own. It needs a collective response and sense of urgency to crack on with it. And when it is offered to teachers in the right way, what we find is that there is a renewed excitement about the teaching of texts in particular, and curriculum design in general. There are very few books that set out the rationale and include examples for professionals to get to work straightaway. *Opening Doors to Ambitious Primary English* is one of them.

We simply can't ignore examples of impact like this:

> As teachers became more proficient in applying the Opening Doors approach, we found that their choices became more ambitious. At Ravenfield Primary Academy, children in Year 6 compared and analysed the language choices within a range of historical speeches from Shakespeare and Elizabeth I to Winston Churchill. Archaic language and motivational aspects were carefully unpicked to enable the children to understand the context and meaning. Taster drafts allowed them to manipulate language from across the speeches, sparking their imagination to create motivational battle speeches of their own.

The proof of any substantive theory – in this case, the offer of demanding texts, including non-fiction and poetry for all pupils – is in what pupils 'produce'. In working in this way, pupils get better not just at reading, but also speaking, listening and writing. Most importantly, they fall in love with beautiful texts too. When you have a resource like *Opening Doors to Ambitious Primary English*, which provides you with the theory, text examples, link texts, concept development, ways of working in the classroom, case studies from schools, all the way through to examples of pupils' work, it makes such logical sense, that you will finish reading it and want to get cracking immediately!

As Bob Cox says, 'I have seen lots of lessons where teachers try to elicit responses from pupils on easily accessible texts. The answers given tend to be monosyllabic right or wrong replies and are less about dialogic responses. No one has done anything wrong, but there was simply not enough scope for learning in the chosen text.' With a resource like this, I am convinced we can do better.

Mary Myatt, education writer, speaker and curator of Myatt & Co

Foreword by Sonia Thompson

When Bob Cox came to St Matthew's Research School, it was like meeting the owner of the most wondrous literary emporium. His love of both classic and contemporary poetry and prose, and the possibilities they offer – not just beautiful writing outcomes but for enabling our children to appreciate beautiful writing – engulfed the hall. The session left us feeling that we needed to be even more courageous with our English curriculum, and we quickly began our journey to empowering our children to widen and deepen their knowledge of a more diverse range of authors and poets.

The crux of the 'Opening Doors' books is that they are like no other educational textbook. Their identity and purpose is truly enshrined within their name. They take the teacher by the hand and lead them on a journey of exploration. *Opening Doors to Ambitious Primary English* builds on this concept by offering the explanations, plans and case studies that enable these ambitious explorations to happen. It answers questions, offers challenge and enables diverse and ambitious literacy to become the norm within your setting. As you turn every page, teachers and English leads may rest assured that every word has been carefully and passionately curated by Bob and his amazing team. That is the beauty of the Opening Doors books.

Exposing our children to high-quality texts is like giving them a gift. Once unwrapped, the opening up of their imagination, through the power of words and illustrations, is a sight to behold. For me, this literary gifting should never be the preserve of the favoured few. I am wholly convinced that it must be available to every child, regardless of circumstance. *Opening Doors to Ambitious Primary English* will not disappoint. There is more richness, more depth and even more literary gold.

Sonia Thompson, head teacher/director, St Matthew's Church of England Primary Research and Support School

Contents

Contents

Contents

Acknowledgements

Our partners

Opening Doors to Ambitious Primary English is all about impact in classrooms, so this isn't just a list of acknowledgement and thanks but a way of highlighting the schools and organisations that have worked with us – and each other – to develop ambitious English as a norm in their communities.

We can only mention some of you here, but the collaborations made represent thousands of teachers and educationists intent on building equity and excellence, not just in words but in their classrooms.

All Saints Church of England Junior School, Fleet, Hampshire

Belmont Academy (LSEAT), Bexleyheath, London

Christ Church Upper Armley Church of England Primary School, Leeds, West Yorkshire

Coastlands County Primary School, St Ishmael's, Pembrokeshire

Crofton Hammond Infant School, Fareham, Hampshire

Four Marks Church of England Primary School, Alton, Hampshire

Frogmore Junior School (GLF Schools), Camberley, Hampshire

Grange Junior School, Farnborough, Hampshire

Hawksworth Wood Primary School, Kirkstall, West Yorkshire

Hook Junior School, Basingstoke, Hampshire

Hordle Church of England Primary School, Lymington, Hampshire

Icknield Primary School, Luton, Bedfordshire

Merdon Junior School, Eastleigh, Hampshire

Mulgrave Primary School, Greenwich, London

Overton Church of England Primary School, Overton, Hampshire

Ravensworth Primary School, Mottingham, London

Red Barn Community Primary School, Portchester, Hampshire

Robin Hood Junior School, Sutton, Surrey

Rossett Acre Primary School, Harrogate, North Yorkshire

Rowner Junior School (Gosport and Fareham Multi-Academy Trust), Gosport, Hampshire

Ryefield Primary School, Uxbridge, London

South Rise Primary School, Greenwich, London

Sparsholt Primary School, Winchester, Hampshire

St Catherine's British School, Athens, Greece

St Matthew's Church of England Primary School, Birmingham, West Midlands

West View Primary School (Ad Astra Academy Trust), Hartlepool, County Durham

Wheatfield Primary School (GLF Schools), Wokingham, Berkshire

Wheatfields Junior School, St Albans, Hertfordshire

Whirley Primary School, Macclesfield, Cheshire

Wyborne Primary School, Greenwich, London

And also:
Ad Astra Academy Trust
Aspire Multi-Academy Trust
Brighter Futures for Children
Greenwich London Borough Council

Herts for Learning
Maltby Learning Trust
National Association for Able Learners in Education
Potential Plus UK
The Potential Trust
River Learning Trust

And:

Crown House Publishing – without whose unstinting interest and skills this book would never have been possible. Thank you!

Straight ahead of oneself, one cannot go very far …

Antoine de Saint-Exupéry, *The Little Prince*

Introduction

The ideas, resources and case studies in this book will help you to make primary English vibrant, creative and challenging in your school. It also provides frameworks and principles for any school wishing to be more ambitious in developing pupils' speaking, listening, reading, writing and thinking. There is an emphasis throughout on application, adaptation to context and links between theory and practice.

Opening Doors to Ambitious Primary English explains and models top quality ways of thinking, planning and teaching which can become a norm in any classroom. It is the opposite of occasionally including an extra challenging unit or offering tricky literary texts to just one group. All pupils have an entitlement to challenging texts, fascinating poetry, or non-fiction in various styles. All pupils can continue to learn about spelling patterns, word derivatives and grammar within the context and beauty of a text. No one should feel excluded and everyone can be aspirational.

How can this be done? We want every teacher reading this book to appreciate that there are numerous creative and fascinating ways in which an English curriculum can be designed to ensure that every single pupil is immersed in rich and diverse literature and language. We want to show how varied learning dialogues and new knowledge planned progressively can be the entitlement of every primary pupil.

Our case studies demonstrate how key principles and a toolkit of techniques can open doors to opportunity via high pitch approaches, with a huge range of access strategies built in. Schools adapt our ideas and feed back to us, creating a genuine knowledge-growing community, one which is focused on rationales and concepts for teaching English. As Eaglestone (2021) observes, 'knowing a discipline is not simply knowing its content, but involves understanding the wider concepts that frame the discipline itself'.

As you turn the pages of this book, you too will become involved in this community as you question, adapt, debate and consider new perspectives. The wonders of a high-quality literary text enable all of us to contribute our own imagination and puzzlement as we work out how best to utilise it to teach our pupils about English language and literature.

Chapter by chapter, we seek to show how ideas and texts – pitched high but accessed by all – can become part of the everyday diet of the classroom. Ambition is rightly admired as a tangible ethos in schools and is often visible via displays, assemblies, websites and aspirational messages, but where ambition is actually fulfilled is in the quality of the teaching in the lessons themselves. We have seen astonishing writing and improved comprehension when teachers have fully exploited the opportunities that challenging texts offer all pupils.

You can dip into any section in your own way. You will notice many cross-references to other chapters, because understanding language development is more of a cognitive field rather than a linear progression. However, we would advise reading Chapter 1 first as it provides the background for the rest of the book. After that, you can follow a narrative from big principles to strategies and specific applications via the chapter headings. This book is all about providing explanations and case studies which explore how top-class primary English can be designed and delivered to every pupil. There is a continuous emphasis on inclusion – for example, strategies like taster drafts offer the potential to deliver spelling, punctuation and grammar in context.

The teaching and learning of English is much more coherent when scaffolded around quality literature. In this way, pupils can be taught, for instance, how to build suspense, what a metaphor is or how connotations spin wildly in our brains, rather than simply 'doing' a book, 'covering' a poem or ticking an assessment box. Above all, we and our schools model how the reading of quality texts can be linked explicitly into the curriculum instead of being marginalised. It is a matter of social justice and equal opportunity that children access a wide range of books from past to present, from across the globe and from picture books to classic literature.

It is you, the teacher, who makes the difference, who intervenes with that much-needed support and scaffolding, who inspires, who cares and who laughs with your pupils. High-quality English texts offer so many more openings for this to happen.

The ideas and examples in this book have been inspired by education research, case studies from the Opening Doors network, the application of Opening Doors strategies and principles, and the combined knowledge of the four educationists who have written the book. There are already 80 units from the five previous books in the 'Opening Doors' series which may interest you too.

From the start, our aim has been to show that pupils enjoy fresh literary challenges more than the standard texts, and this can make the Key Stage 3 programme of study simply the next stepping stone in their reading journey rather than an intimidating step up. We hope you will come away more confident that there are clear route-ways to ambitious English for you and your pupils, and that you can adapt our principles and strategies into a highway to excellence that suits your school.

It is our belief that pupils respond well to high expectations. The key – as we have seen over our long careers – is the difference that a great teacher makes. When excellent ideas are disseminated across a school, local authority or trust as guiding principles, *not* dogma, teachers have the autonomy and freedom to apply strategies as they see fit – and that is confidence-building for a career!

Enjoy opening the doors to opportunity for your pupils, and be inspired by schools like Icknield Primary in Luton, where Lisa Kennedy and Laura McGeachie have recently set up their own training hub:

> At Icknield Primary School, we continue to be excited and motivated by the opportunities our Opening Doors journey affords to both our children and staff. Through visits to other schools to share practice and regular INSETs to refresh and develop key ideas and approaches, our curriculum continues to be enriched. The successes we have experienced thus far have inspired us to share our journey with others: we are in the process of becoming an Opening Doors hub, which will hopefully enable us to spread the word and facilitate mutual support between schools who are genuinely searching for excellence.

Our vision of continuing professional development (CPD) is one that involves us, as writers and educationists, as sign-posters, so that schools like Icknield spread their inspiration further afield. Across the UK, workshop leaders and teaching and learning leaders for trusts and local authorities are exploring the key principles, pedagogies and tools which are making primary-phase English exciting and accessible.

All of the key texts referenced and illustrations featured support your work in the classroom and can be downloaded at: www.crownhouse. co.uk/opening-doors-ambitious-primary-english.

Part 1

Key Opening Doors Principles

Chapter 1

Pitching High and Including All

Bob Cox

The research strongly suggests that it is good to find learning difficult – within reason. We may, in fact, be more likely to remember difficult concepts that we have had to grapple with, puzzle through, or work hard to understand initially than easier ones.

Megan Mansworth, *Teach to the Top:*
***Aiming High for Every Learner* (2021)**

In an ambitious English curriculum, high pitch and high expectation approaches should be visible in every resource and in the sequencing of units. They are integral to all of the ways in which doors can open for your pupils. Dr Megan Mansworth's quote above condenses much of what we encourage and what we see in schools that are committed to challenge for all – that difficulty, once embraced, leads to strengthened memory and understanding. There is nothing more fulfilling than grappling with new concepts under the guidance of a great teacher.

You will learn more about the concept of using concepts as you read this book. There is no definitive list of such concepts in English, but imagine you are teaching an aspect of English rather than 'doing' a text. You might want to teach how to build tension, how structure has supported meaning or how effective personification has enhanced the beauty of a poem. All of these concepts can enhance your attempts to pitch high – for example, you can teach tension-building by using a simpler part of the text with one pupil and a challenging part with another, but *every* child is learning about tension.

Highlights from high expectations history

In a long career spanning many years and various contexts, I have found the phrase 'high expectations' to be a constant presence in the educational landscape. In the 1980s, when the national curriculum was introduced, the advice around so-called differentiation was to teach to the top and not the middle. It wasn't always interpreted in this way, and it jump-started a long process in which lesson planning sometimes distilled the high pitch moments into a discrete 'extension' box, diluting the depth of learning for those outside the targeted group who never reached the extension. The debate continues today in a different form, with 'age-related expectations' interpreted by some as a quality standard around which a teacher can be partly assessed and by others as a guideline above which a lesson should always be pitched.

By 2001, the National Literacy Strategy was well established in primary schools, but some of the same tensions were still apparent between curriculum coverage (which often occurred in a step-by-step way) and the instinct of teachers to include additional provision, at least for those then termed 'gifted and talented'.[1] Interestingly, the *Key Stage 3 National Strategy: English Department Training* document implied a continuation of the rigour of the strategy into secondary schools:

> The main point to draw out is that our first assumption should be to maintain high expectations of all pupils, and not to trap those working below expectations in permanent remediation and those who can go beyond expectations working only to expectations of the average. (Department for Education and Employment, 2001: 97)

---

1   There was a strong government-led initiative via the National Strategies to create gifted and talented coordinators and to disseminate ideas and resources suitable for more able pupils, both in the classroom and through enrichment activities. At one point, schools were asked to identify 10% of their cohort as 'gifted' (which was academic) or 'talented' (in sport and the arts). Of course, both the wording and the rationale have been much disputed ever since!

In 2006, the renewed primary framework for literacy and mathematics implied that more emphasis was needed on challenging expectations. Changes included:

- create a clearer set of outcomes to support teachers and practitioners in planning for progression in literacy and mathematics, to help raise the attainment of all children, personalise learning and secure interventions for those children who need it
- bring an increased sense of drive and momentum to literacy and mathematics through the primary phase, involving some scaling up of expectations and a greater focus upon planning for progression (Department for Education and Skills, 2006: 2)

These ideas had no doubt been influenced by David Miliband's (2004) speech on the future of teaching, in which he said: 'I want to see an education system that combines excellence and equity.'

Changing governments tend to bring changing emphases, but it is noticeable how many theorists and researchers have regularly returned to this theme of high pitch planning. Doug Lemov, Colleen Driggs and Erica Woolway in *Reading Reconsidered* (2016: 5), list 'read harder texts' and 'close read texts rigorously and intentionally' as the first two essential ideas in distilling the 'core of the core' curriculum. Mary Myatt, in *Back on Track* (2020a), consistently emphasises depth, quality texts and high pitch approaches in which every child must be included. The case studies in this book are testament to the many ways in which schools have made the transition from theory to practice, using the scope that complex texts can give.

Opening doors for every child

The principles and strategies in this book will guide you towards an approach that suits you and your school. There are key points in each chapter which will stimulate your thinking, but there are some vital mindsets and strategies that I have observed across schools:

- School leaders believe a challenging curriculum is the entitlement of all pupils and take action to make this happen.

- Governors and teaching and learning leaders from the trust or local authority support school improvement, not just school organisation. An excellence ethos is encouraged.

- CPD is provided which explores subject-specific details and approaches. Some schools have digested principles around high aspirational thinking very well, but they have not engaged in how different disciplinary knowledge is needed for different subjects – for example, what an excellence for all approach looks like in science as compared with English.

- Coaching advice complements exciting curriculum developments to assist the knowledge acquisition and learning of teachers. This isn't connected with performance management.

- Teachers' ongoing reading of literature and mastery of the texts they use is integral to high pitch work. The deeper the knowledge of the teacher, the less planning is needed and the more confidence grows.

- A clear action plan is devised for approximately one to two years – with periodic evaluation – to highlight the rationale for an ambitious curriculum and stages for achievement.

I have been privileged to see many teachers discover the joy and scope that challenging texts offer for daily learning. It might be a picture book with a fascinating concept, like a wall which apparently offers protection from enemies on the other side, as in John Agee's *The Wall in the Middle of the Book*, or the remarkable variation on fairy tale and myth in Andri Snær Magnason's *The Casket of Time*, where the language, style and sheer invention of the text itself offers opportunities for new learning. Perhaps use Victoria Cox's illustration for

Miroslav Holub's 'Fairy Tale' (at the beginning of this chapter) with your pupils and pitch the learning high.[2]

Texts and how teachers use them are the hub around which English as a subject can be delivered. Comprehension, fluency, vocabulary explorations, reading to writing routes and oracy are all enhanced via the scope and power of a complex text.

High pitch for social justice

Pitching high but including all is about social justice too. How can anyone justify leaving any child out of introductions to great literature or relegating them at an early age to discrete, easy work and the labelling that goes with it?

This issue is not new, as we can see in this extract from the Bullock Report into the teaching of language:

The National Child Development Study [Davie et al., 1972] revealed that 48 per cent of the children from social class V were poor readers at 7, compared with 8 per cent in social class I. Several studies have shown that the position worsens as the children grow older, there being a progressive decline in the performance of children of lower socio-economic groups between the ages of 7 and 11. (Bullock, 1975: 22)

Or, more recently, in 2021, in the observations of Jonathan Doherty from Leeds Trinity University on levelling the playing field and promoting social mobility through education:

Social class is the strongest predictor of life outcomes in this country.

From a poor start, the next hurdles appear soon after. In Teach First's 2017 report, *Impossible*, we learn that by age 11, 35% of pupils from low-income backgrounds achieve the expected standards in reading, writing and maths, compared with 57% of their better-off peers.

---

2   You can find the poem at: https://gallimaufry.typepad.com/blog/2016/06/fairy-tale-by-miroslav-holub.html!

> The Education Policy Institute (2017) reported that, at the current rate of progress, it would take 50 years to have an education system where disadvantaged students did not fall behind their peers in formal education up to age 16. (Doherty, 2021: 23–24)

The wording and style changes but the dilemma remains the same. Most importantly, those pupils who find literacy hardest and whose reading scores are low must be included on the journey, and those already displaying very high learning potential need inspiration too: 'Cognitive challenge will prompt and stimulate extended and strategic thinking, analytical and evaluative processes. Pupils will develop these skills more rapidly and learn more effectively when cognitive challenge is distinctive, embedded, and consistent' (National Association for Able Children in Education, 2020: 16).

Two other organisations consistently pioneering for an education system that promotes high-performance learning are Potential Plus, which links with parents and supplies advice and resources,[3] and the Potential Trust, which supports organisations whose ethos embraces top-level challenge.[4]

If you want to take your school on to the global stage with high-performance learning, search out the work of Deborah Eyre (2011, 2016), who has developed networks across the world to share ambitious practice. Denise Yates (2022) is another excellent source of information on pupils with special needs who have high learning potential (or pupils with dual exceptionalities).

If there is one thing I am proud of as our schools open doors across the world, then it is promoting the need for increased access for every child to an enriching and challenging curriculum via a toolkit of strategies. It is so much more stimulating than resorting to easy work as a universal panacea when a pupil is struggling to understand, or to the denial of cognitive challenge to pupils for whom it is as much a necessity as physical exertion and accomplishment might be to others.

---

3   See https://potentialplusuk.org.
4   See https://www.thepotentialtrust.org.uk.

Dr Megan Mansworth (2021: 105) concludes her excellent guide to aspirational teaching, *Teach to the Top*, in this way:

Teaching to the top is also, crucially, a belief that all students deserve to be taught about challenging concepts and ideas. It is an inclusive vision for social justice because when we teach to the top for every student, we empower all students to believe they have the right to access any type of knowledge.

Key points on pitching high

The following chapters will give you a range of principles and strategies from which to select some richer and more ambitious approaches. There is never just one way. As you read this book, you will have an opportunity to discover new methodologies and apply new pedagogies in your context. We are contributing to an ongoing debate about what kind of approaches we need to employ to teach English well.

As you browse, bear in mind the following key points for making high pitch thinking a day-to-day reality in English:

Use *harder texts as a norm* and they will eventually cease to seem harder to you or your pupils.

Use harder texts for *reading aloud and improving fluency.*

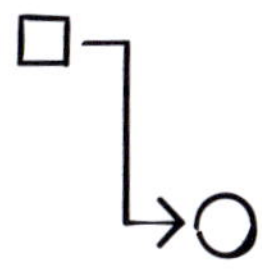

Continually self-reflect and engage with others and in CPD sessions on the *impact evidence* coming from your lessons. Evaluate periodically using your school's performance indicators rather than simply ticking boxes and delivering a set package.

 *Chunk stages of knowledge acquisition.* This makes complex texts manageable to the memory. Harder concepts may actually stick more reliably because of the hard thinking, talking and repeating of notions that the mind has committed to them.

 *Introduce access strategies at every stage* according to need (see Chapter 5). This includes a range of productive group work and oracy skills development.

 Use your skills and knowledge to see the *potential in a rich text*, or even in a few words, for teaching an aspect of English in a deep way.

 Use *excellent models of writing* from past to present, from across the globe, from picture books to contemporary literature and from classic texts to poetry.

 *Link whole-text reading* via concepts or themes and inspire new reading journeys for every child via a system to facilitate it (see Chapter 6).

Case study: The impact of high pitch approaches

Michelle Crawford, West View Primary School, Hartlepool, County Durham

For us, at West View Primary School, it all began in 2019 when our trust, Ad Astra, invited me and our English lead to attend some English training, where Bob Cox's 'going deeper' strategies were introduced.

At first, we were wary and many questions arose: would our special educational needs and disability (SEND) children be able to access this level of challenge? Would the gap become wider? Would our children be able to resonate with these archaic texts? However, after teaching our first unit, 'The Torpor of Death':

The Haunted Hotel by Wilkie Collins, our children were hooked and enthralled! The glass ceiling to learning had been removed and all children, no matter their ability or background, were accessing the great literature set before them.

After 14 years of teaching, I was finally starting to see a change in their attitude towards writing. The children were no longer afraid to put pencil to paper; instead they were itching to get started. I quickly discovered that this approach to excellence in writing was not just for greater depth pupils but about creating a culture of excellence for all. Alongside that, not only had we developed a love of writing in school, but there was also a love of reading. Many children who often avoided reading in class were beginning to ask for book recommendations.

By immersing our pupils in quality texts, we were able to delve deeper to gain a better understanding of vocabulary. The children were then able to experiment with these new words, building their confidence and developing personal flair in their own writing, whilst taking inspiration from great writers of the past. Not only were the children broadening their experiences of literature but we were too as educators: we were teaching texts we had never dreamed of using before. From the start, expectations were high and the children rose to the challenge.

The impact and outcomes in writing are clear to see:

Lizzie awoke restless, breathing heavily – knowing her room was not in utter darkness. This was all perplexing! There was no breeze from the window, no draught from under the door. A vague sense of fear filled her mind.

Cassidy Draper

At an instantaneous moment, Jake woke up wondering how or why he had come to his senses instead of staying in his slumber. His eyes darted left and right; all he could see was the prevailing darkness consuming the objects in the room.

Noah Coates

Resource 2

Chapter 2
Challenge and Response

Bob Cox

Poems are a mid-way point between poets and readers. The poet pours in one set of meanings. The reader picks up the poem and puts in another set of meanings, and the two meet somewhere in the middle.

Michael Rosen, *What is Poetry?* (2016)

Michael Rosen's quote may be about poetry but it surely applies to all texts: the appeal of the writing prises open the potential of the response. The teacher's knowledge and skill activates the process.

The depth of opportunity for pupil responses arises directly from the richness of meaning and ambiguity that a teacher has signalled around an ambitious text and the surfacing of prior reading experiences as connections are made. Challenging texts offer route-ways from curiosity to knowledge to familiarity and even to love of the writing. Practise reading aloud some text yourself several times, roll the words around your tongue and your mind, ask questions about the structure of the words and about their derivation (their morphology and etymology). If you can own the text utterly, then presenting it in class will seem less of a risk.

If a text is too easily accessed by your pupils, the learning process may become cosy – a pleasant journey, perhaps, but one neatly packaged for teaching to the middle. Something will be achieved, but this book tells a story of schools going much deeper with their pupils.

How can prior reading be a springboard for questioning and response?

If you can exploit your own confidence with a challenging text, then you will be able to elicit a range of responses from your pupils which will engage them with key aspects of meaning and keep open the possibility of the unpredictable. This is where an appreciative response can make a powerful alliance with direct transmission. It isn't one or the other; it is a learning partnership. Think back to the Michael Rosen quote: how does a phrase hit our imagination? How much does prior reading and comprehension condition our response? To what extent can a knowledgeable teacher step in with tuition and further questions?

Zoe Helman and Sam Gibbs, in their very thoughtful book *The Trouble with English and How to Address It* (2022: 9), explore authenticity and exam needs. I love their very genuine statement:

Our appreciation might be instinctive, it might not make sense, it might be 'wrong' in the sense that how we've responded is unlikely to be an accurate interpretation of what the author was really thinking. This is rather beautiful. Our strange instincts and the somewhat inexplicable and deeply personal connections we make are the reason many of us love literature.

The effective teacher takes the odd or muddled but thoughtful comment from a pupil and refines it into a deeper search for meaning by adding questions, explanations and summaries, as appropriate. None of this needs to be planned beforehand; all that is required is a confident mastery of the text and a firm grasp of the rationale for teaching it. The deeper the teacher's knowledge, the less planning is required.

Try starting a sequence of knowledge-building about associations with an open question around the illustration at the beginning of this chapter, which is inspired by an extract from *Tamarind and the Star of Ishta* by Jasbinder Bilan, such as: 'What key images do you notice in the picture?' or 'Does this picture remind you of any scenes in stories you have read?' You could then move in from a global question to a more focused one: 'What might the huge arch signify?'

If the sequence utilises sticky notes – with pupils pinning questions and puzzlements about the text onto sugar paper, always with follow-up advice – then you are already beginning to teach the meaning-making behind the connotations in our minds as we read. You could then read out the following passage, perhaps with some sentences repeated by the pupils. Not only is fluency improved in this way, but you can also link the quality of the reading to the meaning of the language.

The sky above us brightens and a full moon spreads jagged shadows across the snow-capped mountains in the distance.

There in front of me, lit up by moonbeams, is a crumbling stone archway smothered in spiralling plants, the entrance to a neglected part of the garden. On top of the arch is a worn statue of a majestic looking woman, standing tall with vast wings behind her. To either side sit two stone owls. Her feet are talons and she rests them lightly on two lions who lie beneath her. One hand is raised as if she's beckoning me forward. (Bilan, 2020: 70)

Your pupils will learn about connotation and narrative style (see Chapter 3) and about connections between words – for example, the dereliction of the garden compared with the regality of the statue. Why might owls be important, and what might they represent? Ask the children what they notice that seems interesting, what key points they would like to note down in their books and what questions they would like to ask. It might look something like this:

Noticed	**Noted**	**Not sure**
Archway sounds like an entrance.	What excited me was what might lie through the archway.	Why are the talons resting *lightly*?

Noticed	Noted	Not sure
Smothered could be a total immersion.		Why is the garden neglected? What does a neglected garden make me think of as a reader?
Lions and owls are common creatures in literature. I think of Aslan.		

You can extend the noticed, noted and not sure exercise further by, for example, forming groups to tackle some of the 'not sure' points and working in strictly timed sessions to suggest meanings or find examples of connotation in the link reading (see Chapter 6). Other groups could imitate the style of the passage in a taster draft to predict what might lie beyond the archway.

After the pupils feed back, you can add any additional teaching points on connotation. In this way, you are maximising what the children can think through and conclude themselves, and then supplementing this with key points of learning or knowledge that they might miss or misunderstand. You are also making the most of your authority by delivering key learning messages in an environment where the pupils are ready to listen since they are already engaged proactively.

I have seen lots of lessons where teachers try to elicit responses from pupils on easily accessible texts. The answers given tend to be monosyllabic right or wrong replies and are less about dialogic responses. No one has done anything wrong, but there was simply not enough scope for learning in the chosen text.

As your familiarity with your own materials grows, you will develop the ability to start setting up both oral and written responses. You can then feel your way to an Opening Doors big question like the one below:

What kind of garden does Jasbinder Bilan describe?

The big question signals the beginning of the long journey to understanding, but it also enables you to chunk out the stages of comprehension and response for your pupils. For example:

* Explore the meaning of 'archway'. What might it signify?

* List the words associated with the statue. Can you see any links in meaning?

* Why are the 'spiralling plants' included?

* What associations do you have with owls and lions?

* What other literary gardens do you know about? Are they similar to or different from the garden Tamarind is in?

Each question is challenging in itself (if necessary, teachers can add easier supplementary questions), but there are routes to meaning and improving reading all the way through.

This text would be perfect for taking pupils beyond the literal and overt meanings found in an adventure story to experiences of symbolism and connotation, without losing the narrative flow that comes from an exciting story.

Professor Robert Eaglestone, in *Literature: Why It Matters* (2019: 10), calls for literature as a 'living conversation': 'Just like a conversation, your creative response to literature draws on your mind, heart, feelings, your past and hopes for the future.'

You can set challenging questions to encourage pupils to explore deeper objectives and responses. For instance, all five questions listed above represent stages in understanding the author's descriptive power, so two further in-depth objectives could take shape:

* How well can you demonstrate an understanding of how the author describes the garden?

* How well can you write a descriptive piece about your own specific setting?

If you define expected outcomes in a way that is too precise or too limiting, then you may inadvertently create an artificial ceiling. By using the question stem 'How well can you …?' and visualising a potential continuum line of response, you are setting a more ambitious expectation. This strategy can be seen in action in *Opening Doors to a Richer English Curriculum for Ages 6 to 9* and *Opening Doors to a Richer English Curriculum for Ages 10 to 13*.

James Durran (2021), a local authority adviser in North Yorkshire, has written an excellent blog post about key learning questions, which you may find useful.[1]

Why is the layout of questions important?

Key questions can be presented in the form of a radial layout (see Chapter 10) and then distributed to individuals and groups as appropriate.

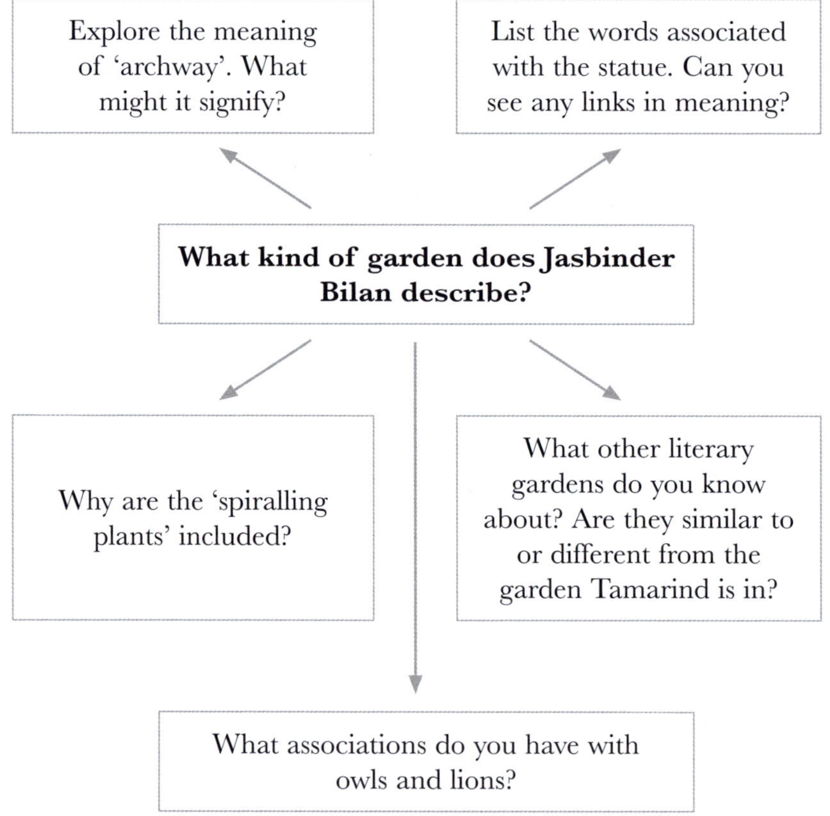

Notice how different the questions seem and how it sets you up for a step-by-step mastery approach. The layout emphasises that each

---

1 See https://jamesdurran.blog/2021/08/28/key-learning-questions-an-introduction.

question is a fascinating springboard in its own right, but that there is also a powerful underlying purpose: all the responses will eventually feed into the pupils successfully answering the big question. (Chapter 9 on excellence success criteria shows how supplementary questions can be used to support a layering of detailed aspects of the chosen concept for the teaching of English). It is a reading journey that features practice and new language interactions en route rather than as a list of comprehension skills exercises.

The quality of the children's responses will be linked to the quality of the dialogic talk in your classroom. Whether the pupils discuss questions in groups, with talking partners or as a whole class, you are encouraging informed responses that have grown from your own mastery and teaching of the text coupled with your pupils' prior reading and learning habits in the classroom. The question box about other literary gardens could be used as a 'greater depth' challenge for those pupils advanced enough on the big question to attempt. However, it may not be necessary to label it as such because an enriched curriculum is for everyone, and you may be surprised just how many pupils are ready to make deeper connections.

Your pupils' observations may well be the highlight of your lesson and a source of genuine delight. Take the 'spiralling plants' question, for example, which might produce comments about winding growth or a link with the meaning of 'smothered'. Some children may associate the word 'spiralling' with being out of control. Emotional responses are vital too. This text could elicit feelings around mythology, religion, derelict sites, spooky gardens or anything else gloriously unknown. Each comment can provide you with a way in – a pathway to how an individual has engaged with meaning.

Gradually, your pupils will pick up new knowledge, understanding and skills from each supplementary question and build towards applying their ideas to the big question. The depth and detail in your teaching will embed the learning about description and connotation, which the pupils will then be ready to transfer into their own creative writing.

Eaglestone (2019: 9–10) explores a range of studies on the rationale for literature and makes a number of enlightening assertions about the importance of the reader's response: 'Literature isn't just about the books on the shelf: it's about you thinking, responding, writing about, talking with the books too.' I particularly like *talking with* – and the *you* is all of us! If we, as educators, can encourage the voice of our pupils to live and grow in our classrooms, then we enhance the chances of them becoming lifelong readers.

How can challenging texts increase the depth of response?

Until you have asked the children for responses about meaning, it is impossible to know how many of them have the prior reading and knowledge necessary to grasp the nuance found in some descriptions. Too often, meaning is skimmed over and left unexplored or passages aren't selected because they are deemed to be too hard.

Let us suppose there is no response at all from your class to the meaning of 'spiralling'. This is when you would adapt your approach and present it in a different way, perhaps injecting more knowledge and explanations, like visuals of spiralling plants and other examples of winding patterns like staircases.

Consequently, even a blank response can lead indirectly to deeper learning because it provides you with information that can help you to adapt your curriculum and priorities accordingly. The pupils' responses – or lack thereof – alert you to the need either to explain a concept in a different way or to ask easier questions, but you should only resort to this when your challenging questions encounter genuine bafflement and not simply a reluctance to think hard.

A challenge too far?

Finally, your pioneering may reveal that a text really is too hard. The difficulty may come from sophisticated wordplay, a cultural backdrop needing a mature reader's eye or confusing vocabulary. Some books are inappropriate for primary pupils because of their content, and we are not suggesting that pupils should do anything other than wait until they are older for exposure to young adult themes.

What I will say is that our schools have had huge success using extracts from, for example, *The Woman in White* by Wilkie Collins and *Wuthering Heights* by Emily Brontë (both of which feature in the 'Opening Doors' series) and scenes from Shakespeare. To experience, for instance, the description of Miss Havisham from *Great*

Expectations by Charles Dickens is an entitlement for all, and a vital stepping stone to engaging with wider literature. Such texts can make the Key Stage 3 curriculum joyful rather than intimidating.

Using extracts doesn't make an extract culture. It isn't about encouraging a diet that is limited to snippets, but supporting the exploration of language that all pupils can understand and commit to memory without being overwhelmed. Our schools teach literacy in a focused way via zooming in on the style and beauty of the writing, but they always link it with whole-text reading on similar concepts (for more on link reading see Chapter 6). The learning gleaned from extracts actually accelerates whole-text experiences, but there is no pressure to read the whole of *Great Expectations* for a while yet! Of course, the occasional child will try to do so of their own choosing for pleasure and without any adult pushing them on. That is because we are all different, and reading for pleasure will mean different things to different pupils.

We should be teaching into the gaps of understanding and using challenging texts to reveal where those gaps are. For example, if pupils find it difficult to understand the impact and importance of connotation, then it is an indication that more specific teaching, modelling and exploration is required. In the past, these pupils have been omitted from the learning, relegated to different tables and given easy (and sometimes condescending) work, but it is more than possible to include them. The strategies we describe in this book – like taster drafts, the chunking of knowledge acquisition, radial layouts, visuals and easier questions (but about the same rich text) – all contribute to equity and excellence.

Schools often deepen pupils' understanding of a concept like connotation by drawing on 20 or 30 link texts, incorporating connections and responses from a wide range of reading matter – a true tapestry of intertextuality. These texts can be very different, but each will provide an opportunity to teach in an ambitious way and for each pupil to find an appropriate route-way.

Natalie Wexler, the author of *The Knowledge Gap* (2019), writing in a blog for *Forbes* states: 'reading comprehension is different. It's not just a *reading* process. It's inextricably connected to the process of learning in general. And cognitive scientists have found that the key factor in learning new information is how much relevant information you already have' (Wexler, 2022b). It is the systematic link reading expectations that boost that 'relevant information' for every child.

Link reading

You will find the following units from the 'Opening Doors' series useful in linking connotation work with *Tamarind and the Star of Ishta*:

- *Alice's Adventures in Wonderland* by Lewis Carroll (Unit 11 in *Opening Doors to Famous Poetry and Prose*)

- 'Lonely Street' by Francisco López Merino (Unit 8 in *Opening Doors to Quality Writing for Ages 6 to 9*)

- *The Phantom Coach* by Amelia B. Edwards (Unit 2 in *Opening Doors to Quality Writing for Ages 10 to 13*)

- 'The Frost, the Sun and the Wind' (Russian folk tale translated by Charles Downing) (Unit 9 in *Opening Doors to a Richer English Curriculum for Ages 6 to 9*)

- 'The Door in the Wall' by H. G. Wells (Unit 10 in *Opening Doors to a Richer English Curriculum for Ages 10 to 13*)

These suggestions should also inspire your pupils:

- *The Night Gardener* by Eric and Terry Fan

- *A House That Once Was* by Julie Fogliano

- *The Little Prince* by Antoine de Saint-Exupéry

Key points on eliciting response

Master the text yourself by rereading, underlining your own puzzlements, exploring with colleagues and gradually reading some of the link texts. Your *confidence will grow the more you read the texts* and the more you use the texts for teaching.

 Use a range of *access strategies* (see Chapter 5) including extracts or even slivers of texts. The challenge of the text will provide scope for new knowledge to grow, and all pupils can be given ways into the wonder of the words.

 Take a *step-by-step approach* to questioning and knowledge acquisition so that pupils' responses can grow incrementally.

 Apply a range of *dialogic talk* to elicit oral responses. Use thinking engines and radial question layout structures as frameworks through which pupils' responses can deepen (see Chapter 8).

 Immerse pupils in the curriculum through *quality texts with links to quality writing*. The depth and range of the responses will help to make those links.

Case study: Responding to the challenge of link reading

Kathy Whitford, Merdon Junior School, Eastleigh, Hampshire

Linked texts are intrinsic in all of the Opening Doors units and provide the opportunity to deepen and broaden children's reading experiences, often offering opportunities to compare and contrast poems and texts, so why not use the Opening Doors texts to make similar links in your wider curriculum?

For example, pupils in Year 6 study the Second World War, with an emphasis on children and how their lives were affected by the war. They study *Goodnight Mister Tom* by Michelle Magorian and *Once* by Morris Gleitzman, as well as being given the opportunity to read a range of fiction and non-fiction books during the half term.

'The Companion' by Yevgeny Yevtushenko was recommended as a poem that would make this link: https://internetpoem.com/yevgeny-yevtushenko/the-companion-poem.

The big question was: 'How does Yevtushenko use first-person narrative to build impressions of children in wartime?'

We began to introduce the narrative poem and the characters within it through slow reveal, starting with the first four lines. Further extracts from the poem can then be used to make inferences about character, setting and emotion based on what we learn about 'the girl'. During the process, the children considered: how do the clothes reflect the girl's situation? How is the story told and through whose eyes? Irony was tracked in the way the boy apparently feels superior to girls, but it is the girl who subsequently helps him with the boots.

Taster drafts were completed at different stages, giving the children an opportunity to respond through poetry or prose. The children used a range of Opening Doors strategies, including mark and note, dialogic talk and think, pair, share.

The final writing outcome was to create a narrative poem depicting the journey of Zelda and Felix across war-torn Poland, using *Once* by Morris Gleitzman as the inspiration:

She was lying on the burnt, bloody grass,

a round bruise on the left of her forehead.

The house beaming beside her,

drying my tears.

Her parents had passed.

No holes had appeared in her pyjamas,

I rolled her over, she woke.

I'd no idea what to do with her,

And how I would tell her about her parents.

Ava Bartlett

The girl was weak, he was certain of it.
'Don't you listen?' she'd say. 'I'm hungry' she'd say.
She'd start yelling in no time he was certain of it,
But as things turned out it was he who started yelling.
She growled, she wasn't going any further and she sat
down suddenly on a log.
'What's wrong?' he said.
'Don't cry.'
The train started. The train whistled.
On and on the train went.
Until, finally.
They jumped without thinking,
passing gunshots, passing bodies
under the rocking sky of '42,
vibrating the ground beneath.

Eva Humme

Resource 4

Chapter 3

Text Choice and Concepts

Bob Cox

The reading of a text is an event occurring at a particular time in a particular environment at a particular moment in the life history of the reader.

Louise Rosenblatt, *The Reader, the Text, the Poem* (1978)

Choosing a core text for a unit of work is the most critical decision you will make as a teacher. After all, it is the teacher's raw material for the magical process of transforming language, style and tone into dynamic learning for their pupils.

That being the case, there is a key question to be confronted: how can *this* text be used to teach aspects of English? Answering this question requires in-depth thinking about the potential of the text for learning. Sometimes, schools give more thought to the delivery mode or to the sequencing of the learning in a lesson rather than considering the rationale behind the choice of text. The former requires a mastery of the lesson plan; the latter requires a mastery of the text!

For an ambitious approach to English, consider the differences between the drivers of text choice in the following table:

Enthusiasm	Reading for teaching[1]	Whole-school curriculum design
I love that text. I have seen that on social media. That is on a well-known influencer's reading spine. Great author! Leah Crawford mentioned that text. I read that when I was at school. That is a classic! That fits into our topic.	I can use the complex ideas and techniques in that text for specific teaching and a chosen concept. That text supports my need to improve fluency or an aspect of spelling, punctuation or grammar. I can teach specific comprehension strategies through that text. That text supports my reading for pleasure and challenge policies.	The text progresses well from one used as a core text last term/year. The text has some fascinating ideas on building suspense, which is a Year 4 concept. It may enhance learning compared with the present Year 4 text. The text adds more complexity compared with last term's.

My next piece of advice needs careful explanation. The table suggests what ideas you might consider; it isn't an attempt to say that loving a text doesn't matter. There have been times in my varied career when it has been my delight in the flow and meaning of a text that has maintained my morale in the face of all kinds of blitzes! However, I am saying that it is worth reflecting on the big picture of text choice drivers. Ultimately, the teacher's role is to teach new aspects of English. That may mean reading aloud, questioning, shar-

---

1   By 'reading for teaching', I mean the process by which we come across a text (literary, media, non-fiction or play script) and assess, using our knowledge and skills, how it might be used for teaching an aspect of English.

ing, transmitting and inspiring, but it is the text that provides the opportunity for that to happen.

As Louise Rosenblatt observes, individual pupils will encounter the same text in different ways, but don't forget that you are at a certain stage in your reading and teaching development too. As you reflect more on learning processes, it is logical that you may suddenly see the limitations of a narrative, poem or play script that you have used many times. This doesn't negate the past; when you choose new texts you are upgrading your expectations for your pupils, yourself and your school.

In addition, the personal preferences of your pupils may change as they fall under the spell of an entrancing narrative. We can all remember a teacher who introduced us to some special reading, even though there may have been early reluctance (see Chapter 13 for my exploration of a poem I previously found very irritating!).

Reading for teaching is a career-long process. As you sharpen your instincts for a text, you will become attuned to its scope for ambition, not just content delivery. For example, a poem which has proved very popular is 'The Call' by Charlotte Mew (Unit 1 in *Opening Doors to Famous Poetry and Prose*), yet hardly any of the teachers in our schools had heard of it initially. Both affection and an understanding of how much can be learnt about narrative poetry has grown with usage. These haunting lines often flow through the mind like an echo:

To-night we heard a call,

A rattle on the window-pane,

A voice on the sharp air,

And felt a breath stirring our hair,

I hope you want to read on! Many of our schools find that there is a shift in text choice criteria as thinking on aspirations deepens at meetings and INSETs. There is less talk of 'doing' texts and more on the consideration of sequencing and progression – a school journey towards rigour and transition at Key Stage 3.

What concepts are you teaching via the text?

Mary Myatt, in *Back on Track*, devotes a whole chapter to a passionate consideration of concepts:

> Concepts have a powerful effect on learning. Identifying the big ideas helps pupils to make sense of what they are being taught. Instead of a random list of stuff to be learned, the concept acts as an expandable portmanteau that enables a child to draw on prior knowledge and include new knowledge. The identification and explicit teaching of concepts support pupils to make rich connections. (Myatt, 2020a: 90)

A text might be chosen for teaching irony, melodrama or the effect of repetition, for showing how tension builds or revealing how mystery thickens in a narrative. These concepts provide multilayered possibilities for whole-class teaching with an exciting scope: a rich panorama of literary meaning to be explored and loved rather than a limited curriculum of single unrelated tasks starkly out of context.

Let us take an example of how doors can start opening to exciting English teaching. I fell in love with this passage from the start of *Treasure Island* by Robert Louis Stevenson a long time ago:

> I take up my pen in the year of grace 17__ and go back to the time when my father kept the Admiral Benbow inn and the brown old seaman with the sabre cut first took up his lodging under our roof.
>
> I remember him as if it were yesterday, as he came plodding to the inn door, his sea-chest following behind him in a hand-barrow – a tall, strong, heavy, nut-brown man, his tarry pigtail falling over the shoulder of his soiled blue coat, his hands ragged and scarred, with black, broken nails, and the sabre cut across one cheek, a dirty, livid white. I remember him looking round the cove and whistling to himself as he did so, and then breaking out in that old sea-song that he sang so often afterwards:
>
> 'Fifteen men on the dead man's chest –
>
> Yo-ho-ho, and a bottle of rum!'

Reading for teaching habits can lead to a rapid assessment of a famous passage like this. One approach is to focus on the concept of vivid characterisation development; potential excellence success criteria might include:

- Visual appeal (e.g. 'sabre cut').

- Worn themed adjectives (e.g. 'dirty') and verbs (e.g. 'scarred').

- Exploration of individual vocabulary (e.g. 'livid').

- The contrast of his rough appearance with the confident whistling.

- The content of the sea song.

- The spelling of 'ragged' and 'scarred', for example, which provide opportunities to weave spelling patterns into meanings and contexts. If the words become fascinating, the spelling will be remembered!

For those pupils ready to extend this exploration, they could:

- Think more about the effect of the first-person narrator filtering impressions through to the reader.

- Connect this vivid characterisation with others from a pre-prepared link reading list.

Immediately, the techniques you will have noted – like the use of colours and the pattern of wounded fatigue – can be related to an overall meaning: the characterisation of the old seaman is inferring the arrival of someone from a world of danger and death, notwithstanding the infamous rhyme. The vocabulary exploration will be glorious, and the links with other fictional characters has limitless scope (see Chapter 6). The reading, initially modelled by you, will also contribute to the pupils' comprehension, with fluency developed via the echoing of lines and sections. The meaning is indeed *in* the reading!

You may find the illustration helpful too. As you will find in all the 'Opening Doors' books, Victoria Cox tries to give you opportunities as a teacher to use visual literacy creatively – for example, in questioning:

- What might be in the chest? How can you attempt an answer without guessing or reading on?

- Can you draw the seaman's hand?

❦ What other words could describe the pigtail?

❦ Can you choose and change the adjectives 'tall, strong, heavy, nut-brown'? Can you explain how your vocabulary choices subtly change the meaning and characterisation?

Your own curiosity as a teacher will help to maintain your inspiration throughout the unit, and you will pass this enthusiasm on to your pupils. So, master the text first, link it with a chosen concept, and the questioning and assessment details will follow because they enforce the concept of vivid characterisation. You now have your rationale – the 'why' that drives the learning and deepens the challenge.

Concepts should offer children of all abilities the chance to find appropriate stepping stones, whilst also sharing the power of learning about vivid characterisation together as a whole class. They will need to revisit the material, but it will be applied to harder texts as your pupils move into secondary school. Graham Nuthall, in his highly influential book, *The Hidden Lives of Learners* (2007: 63), gives us some valuable advice: 'We discovered that a student needed to encounter, on at least three different occasions, the complete set of the information she or he needed to understand a concept.' The depth to be found in exploring effective characterisation knows no bounds.

Consider how the use of a challenging text alongside a concept-driven approach can provide teachers with opportunities to layer ambitious learning, whilst also offering challenging routes for all learners. Here is an example:

> What is the immediate impact of 'sabre cut'? Why is 'livid' such an impactful word?

> List and connect the striking and vivid descriptions. How is each one different? How do they form a pattern of impact?

How does Robert Louis Stevenson build vivid characterisation?

> How does the first-person narrator help to reveal the seaman? Try rewriting it in the third person. What difference does it make?

> Find as many other vivid descriptions as you can from the link reading list. Which one is your favourite, and why?

By using radial layouts (see Chapter 10), each step represents new knowledge, which can get progressively harder as the pupils' confidence grows. The concept and the big question give you the chance to stop, reflect and, above all, teach to a group or whole class according to their needs, not to pre-planned labelling. Ambition can be shared by all pupils with enthusiasm, and not fear. This lends focus and purpose to English, and encourages creativity as the pupils gain the knowledge needed to imitate, adapt and imagine when they apply what they have learnt to their own writing.

Other concepts you might like to consider in your discussions include:

- Structure
- Building suspense
- Building argument
- Contextual concepts
- Metaphor
- Effective characterisation

❦ Plot characteristics

❦ Symbolism

You may also be interested in grouping concepts together under topics like structure, which may go deeper. Concepts should be used actively in lessons, explored with pupils and used to form schemas – mental structures in the mind that are used to organise knowledge – which enhance memory and understanding.

Zoe Helman and Sam Gibbs, in *The Trouble with English and How to Address It* (2022: 60), explain the impact that concepts can have: 'We felt that encouraging teachers to think and teach conceptually would mean that important understanding in our subject that sometimes remains hidden or only half-explored, would be made explicit, sequenced carefully and taught deliberately rather than opportunistically.'

Some excellent podcasts on this subject are available via Tiny Voice Talks (@Toriaclaire):

❦ Talk for Reading with Pie Corbett: https://podcasts.apple.com/gb/podcast/talk-for-reading-with-pie-corbett/id1526852152?i=1000551447776

❦ Opening Doors with Bob Cox: https://podcasts.apple.com/us/podcast/opening-doors-with-bob-cox-raising-standards-by/id1526852152?i=1000552764060

Link reading

You will find the following units from the 'Opening Doors' series useful in linking characterisation work with the ideas in *Treasure Island*:

❦ *Great Expectations* by Charles Dickens (Unit 8 in *Opening Doors to Famous Poetry and Prose*)

❦ *The Pavilion on the Links* by Robert Louis Stevenson (Unit 12 in *Opening Doors to Famous Poetry and Prose*)

❦ *Dracula* by Bram Stoker (Unit 13 in *Opening Doors to Famous Poetry and Prose*)

❦ *The Phantom Coach* by Amelia B. Edwards (Unit 2 in *Opening Doors to Quality Writing for Ages 10 to 13*)

- *David Copperfield* by Charles Dickens (Unit 12 in *Opening Doors to a Richer English Curriculum for Ages 10 to 13*)

Examples from children's literature abound, but here are a few with vivid characters:

- The graveyard characters in *The Graveyard Book* by Neil Gaiman

- The Birdman in *Why the Whales Came* by Michael Morpurgo

- Albie Bright in *The Many Worlds of Albie Bright* by Christopher Edge

- Sade in *The Other Side of Truth* by Beverley Naidoo

- The Psammead in *Five Children and It* by Edith Nesbit

Key points on using texts and concepts

The *text choice* should be linked to the rationale for teaching the unit, which should be ambitious in terms of language, style and vocabulary.

The text should have a coherent appeal of its own to which pupils can respond and which *access strategies* will bring alive (see Chapter 5).

The rationale can be expressed in a *concept* which gives multilayered possibilities for all learners to thrive and be enriched.

The concept can *knit together* the core text and the link reading to create connections and cohesion.

The challenge of the text, the learning dialogues that deepen knowledge acquisition and *the focus the concept gives* all contribute to a richer English experience.

Case study: Text choice impact on a whole school

Marcel Penarroja, Wyborne Primary School, Greenwich, London

As part of the COVID-19 recovery programme, Wyborne Primary, as a whole school, read the book *Here We Are* by the celebrated author and illustrator Oliver Jeffers. The upheaval of the pandemic and an ensuing lockdown meant the world (for two years at least) as our children knew it was different than before. Things had changed. School had changed.

Oliver Jeffers created this book as a gift for his son to make sense of the world he had been born into. However, it was a crucial tool for teachers to do the same for the children who returned to us after yet more disruption to their learning.

Although *only* a picture book, the text presented our children with a myriad of writing opportunities. Some of the older children composed poetry, using devices such as similes, metaphors and personification, basing their compositions on the feeling of being 'here' on our planet. Truly, the children learnt what it meant to feel here. A sense of belonging and stability was successfully reinforced when the outside world was far from stable.

In addition, the text beautifully explores the abundance of flora and fauna in our world. Several classes examined the style of narration in nature documentaries, specifically those of David Attenborough. In their link reading, the children became familiar with his style and imagined what he might have said or written. They then created their own play scripts as an end product.

Further down the school, the text afforded an early glimpse into how different we all are and that this diversity should be championed by our early writers at a young age.

Thus, a true sense of belonging to our planet and its peoples was formed throughout the school using a fantastic text which provided many creative avenues for teachers and children to explore.

Now that we have established an understanding of the familiar world around us, we have the opportunity to investigate texts such as *Leon and the Place Between* by Angela McAllister, where reality can suddenly flip into the fantastical and the ephemeral. Alternatively, our starting point could be with different realities entirely, in complex and challenging texts such as Philip Pullman's *Northern Lights* or *The Girl of Ink and Stars* by Kiran Millwood Hargrave.

In writing terms, the world is our oyster, but there is now more on our literary menu.

Resource 6

Chapter 4

Quality Text to Quality Writing

Bob Cox

We also note that children, like adults, demand contemporary literature. The old romance is retold, but not 'exactly in the ancient way'.

***Newbolt Report* (1921)**

In 1921, the Newbolt Report came out. It explored many aspects of education in elementary schools and one was approaches to literature. Wonderful research by one Head Mistress. Not much changes in almost 100 years re: Teachers and Readers (except, perhaps, the reading matter) …

Mat Tobin (2020)[1]

There is a long history of teachers searching for ways of introducing pupils to quality texts, not always successfully: 'Merely to distribute books is not enough; failing some interest shown by the teacher, many children will listlessly turn over the pages and prove to know little about a book they profess to have read' (Newbolt, 1921: 85). The quest for suitable and varied literature – and ways to present it – is ongoing.

Time and again, I have emphasised the importance of the teacher to a child's learning and to the improvement of schools, over and above the latest push for traditional or progressive education, for oracy or direct transmission, for group talk or sitting in rows. A teacher who learns and develops throughout their career understands when to intervene, when to change resources, when to apply new methodologies and when to be conservative: that is experience. These kinds of

---

1   See https://twitter.com/Mat_at_Brookes/status/1223253376974163971. The references to the Newbolt Report are thanks to this tweet by Mat Tobin, a senior lecturer at Oxford Brookes University.

teachers – and the head teachers who grow them – are constantly involved in facilitating reading for pleasure and building reading for challenge in lessons as both a joy and a daily expectation. Their pro-active involvement prevents their pupils from being permitted to listlessly turn pages, and makes them more likely to be the ones asking the questions!

How can the potential of a text be exploited?

Let us take an example using Sue Hardy-Dawson's 'Fog Warning' from the excellent collection *Where Zebras Go* (2017). Here are the first two lines:

Today sky will be heavy in all places
and some streets may be without colour.

We might choose to teach 'image-making' as a concept and explore all sorts of delightful uses of language:

- How can a 'heavy' sky be seen or felt?
- What is a street without colour?
- How would this text be read? How does punctuation support meaning?

Our schools are quick to recognise how the quality of a text can offer the potential to build an appreciation and love of styles, words and phrases, in this case via poetry. Of course, this is a warning about fog, an announcement, so there is additional scope for teaching about imperatives and broadcasts. Where was the warning announced and to whom?

Using concepts like image-making with quality texts has shifted the emphasis away from tick-box approaches or the demand for predictable imitations of specific text types. Learning about a range of concepts and styles throughout the primary phase will equip budding readers and writers with more flexible tools and comprehension strategies, matching styles to audience and purpose.

Here is the full version of 'Fog Warning':

Today sky will be heavy in all places
and some streets may be without colour.

Dew could develop later in hedges
whilst telegraph wires will hang about unseen.

Grey trees will smoulder darkly
and there are strong warnings of muted grass.

It's likely houses may seem patchy.
Expect most riverbanks to appear faded
with high probabilities of willows weeping.

Flowers are advised not to open unless they must
as misty sunlight will tend to be fleeting.

Generally birdsong is going to be hushed
giving little chance for a glimpse of its furtive singers.

Everywhere cobwebs will drip chandeliers.

You will enjoy the reading for teaching here – finding all the knowledge and learning possibilities to use in your creative English classroom! Don't forget to focus on that last line, which, for me, has an eye for detail which will make me go searching for cobwebs the next time it is foggy; amidst the murk and blurred light, there is something utterly beautiful to be seen out there. The adverb 'Everywhere' reads like an imperative, and the final image of a chandelier clinks in the imagination!

I would pause just momentarily before delivering the impact of that final line. Once again, the meaning lies in the reading.

The links between the quality of the poem and the joy of your pupils crafting their own poetry can now begin. Once you have taught and discussed with them the power of figurative language, such as 'smoulder', 'fleeting' or 'furtive singers', you have all sorts of options to elicit quality writing. We advise using these kinds of texts in which there is clever word use and originality but also a high level of accessibility.

Some of the following questions could be used to prompt some thoughtful image-making:

❦ What else could the cobwebs be likened to?

❦ What would your school be like in the fog?

❦ What new things could a fog warning include?

❦ Can you include language that implies a formal warning in your writing?

❦ Can you say more about the 'furtive singers'?

❦ Can you write about the wind arriving and dispersing the fog?

❦ Why is the image of a chandelier used in the last line?

❦ Why does the illustration include a cobweb in each image?

You could also use the illustration imaginatively. The five strips could be cut up and a new line or couplet invented for each image, which could provide a framework for a new poem. Some teachers start with visual literacy explorations before introducing any of the text. So, the cobweb could be used to signpost short taster drafts on cobwebs more generally before the children read 'Fog Warning'.

I often find there is much valuable poetry work going on in the earlier primary years via fun rhymes and a plethora of superb poets. Sue Hardy-Dawson's poetry is ideal in terms of the joy of reading poetry and maintaining access for all, but there is also the potential for adding some more complex wordplay, images and deeper thinking as the children progress through the phase. Think of it as a quality text stepping stone towards upper Key Stage 2 and Key Stage 3.

Let the texts teach the reader

Throughout this book, we exemplify how to tap into the beauty and depth of a quality text. This applies to more accessible texts that are suitable for younger readers, like 'Fog Warning', or more complex texts for older pupils, like 'Ozymandias' (see Chapter 5). Pie Corbett writes a lot about imitation to innovation in his world famous 'Talk for Writing' series, which is a perfect way to link the value of a culture of reading with the ability to keep on improving the quality of writing. Most professional writers reference authors and books that have influenced their own writing development.

Margaret Meek echoes this critical relationship in *How Texts Teach What Readers Learn* (1988: 38): 'One of the sharpest, late reading lessons I have learned is to let the texts teach the reader ... If we want to see what lessons have been learned from the texts children read, we have to look for them in what they write.'

Linking in whole-text reading

Your link reading selections can take the teaching of image-making deeper but still maintain the key theme.

Try this absolute gem of a poem by Carl Sandburg: https://www.poetryfoundation.org/poems/45032/fog-56d2245d7b36c.

Some pupils may be ready for Thomas Hardy's spooky evocation of a head above the fog: http://www.online-literature.com/hardy/moments-of-vision/72. This would be great for macabre and gothic image-making!

Or try comparing and contrasting Sue Hardy-Dawson's images of a fog warning with Valerie Bloom's evocation of frost: https://childrens.poetryarchive.org/poem/frost.

By linking a range of reading into the curriculum (see Chapter 6), you are prioritising and emphasising the vitality of ambitious reading. Why not collect a whole pile of poems on the weather and ask your pupils to browse, read, talk, debate and recite them? Your selection should include a range of language, styles and readability – from Valerie Bloom to Thomas Hardy. You could even include a famous illustration by Gustav Dore alongside a rich discussion on theme and context, which could be matched to a few selected stanzas from Coleridge's 'The Rime of the Ancient Mariner': https://www.bl.uk/collection-items/the-ancient-mariner-illustrations-by-dore.

For a wordless picture book onto which all sorts of language, captions or narratives can be mapped, I would recommend the adventures of a paper boat in *The Wanderer* by Peter Van den Ende.

The profound ideas and abstract concepts that are so vital for learning can be found in picture books as well as in classic texts or contemporary favourites. Perhaps we are edging nearer to a definition of a quality text: reading matter or a visual literacy resource which takes our thinking and wonder deeper and further. After all, I have just suggested a death-in-life character from 'The Rime of the Ancient Mariner', some foggy chandeliers from Sue Hardy-Dawson and a giant spilling icing sugar from Valerie Bloom as a concoction of images that can lead the minds of budding writers into new twists and turns of language: quality text into quality writing.

The reader, the writer and the knowledge

A well-known research project that produced fascinating insights on this topic was set up by the Centre for Literacy in Primary Education, formerly the Centre for Language in Primary Education. In *The Reader in the Writer*, Myra Barrs and Valerie Cork (2001) reported on research in Year 5 classrooms where pupils were introduced to challenging literature as part of teaching literacy. In the preface, Margaret Meek Spencer (2001: 20) states:

> There is a deal of evidence, both quantitative and qualitative, that the literary quality of the texts the children encountered not only played a large part in their success, but also showed them how to enjoy continuous reading and writing as something they could do because they wanted to.

It is vitally important to the Opening Doors team that we see this happening in our schools, and it means everything to teachers too. Reading for challenge so often links with and complements reading for pleasure. I am not sure the two can be parted: independent reading and the journey towards becoming a lifelong reader frequently dovetail with a growing need for something meaty and wondrous, especially when facilitated by a skilful and knowledgeable teacher.

> The most effective teachers have deep knowledge of the subjects they teach, and when teachers' knowledge falls below a certain level it is a significant impediment to students' learning. As well as a strong understanding of the material being taught, teachers must also understand the ways students think about the content, be able to evaluate the thinking behind students'

own methods, and identify students' common misconceptions. (Coe et al., 2014: 2)

What we have seen in our schools, and what we are advocating in this book, is that the number one resource for learning is the reading culture within a staff team. External training should be ambitious enough to stimulate and grow that culture even more. I remember speaking to a teacher who said that the expectation to provide link reading had actually spurred her on to read more herself – a habit that had been sustained. We can look up half-forgotten knowledge on fronted adverbials or the use of capital letters, but it takes time and commitment to build cumulative knowledge about style, genre and meaning. The teacher concerned told me she felt like a more widely read person, and this had improved her overall confidence in herself as an educator and academic.

Take a look at some of the fascinating work by pupils who have been stimulated by the units in the first five 'Opening Doors' books. This is the best evidence of the power of quality text to quality writing journeys. Visit https://www.crownhouse.co.uk/authors/bob-cox and click on each book to find unit titles and examples of pupils' work.

Link reading

All 80 units in the series have quality text to quality writing routes. If you want to follow up more image-making in poetry, try the following:

- ❦ 'The Eagle' by Alfred, Lord Tennyson (Unit 16 in *Opening Doors to Famous Poetry and Prose*)

- ❦ 'Overheard on a Saltmarsh' by Harold Monro (Unit 5 in *Opening Doors to Quality Writing for Ages 6 to 9*)

- ❦ 'Lonely Street' by Francisco López Merino (Unit 8 in *Opening Doors to Quality Writing for Ages 6 to 9*)

- ❦ 'Mementos' by Charlotte Brontë (Unit 9 in *Opening Doors to Quality Writing for Ages 10 to 13*)

- ❦ 'A Garden at Night' by James Reeves (Unit 13 in *Opening Doors to Quality Writing for Ages 10 to 13*)

- ❦ 'Blue Remembered Hills' by A. E. Housman (Unit 14 in *Opening Doors to Quality Writing for Ages 10 to 13*)

- ❦ 'Wind' by Dionne Brand (Unit 1 in *Opening Doors to a Richer English Curriculum for Ages 6 to 9*)

- ❦ 'Dear March – Come In –' by Emily Dickinson (Unit 4 in *Opening Doors to a Richer English Curriculum for Ages 6 to 9*)

- ❦ 'Speak of the North!' by Charlotte Brontë (Unit 2 in *Opening Doors to a Richer English Curriculum for Ages 10 to 13*)

- ❦ 'Cold Mountain' by Han-Shan (Unit 4 in *Opening Doors to a Richer English Curriculum for Ages 10 to 13*)

- ❦ 'A Coloured Print by Shokei' by Amy Lowell (Unit 6 in *Opening Doors to a Richer English Curriculum for Ages 10 to 13*)

Key points on quality text to quality writing routes

Exploit the potential of a text by assessing which aspects of English can be taught and how they can be applied in pupils' writing.

Use the advice from other chapters on taster drafts, concepts and radial layouts to exploit the beauty of the text and start to teach aspects of writing via the application of what the children have learnt. Imitation is what professional writers do – taking models and refining and adapting them. Eventually, a *personal voice* emerges.

Learn from great writers, past and present and from across the globe. *Let the text speak* to you and your pupils; remarkable writing will emerge from this stimulus plus your teaching.

Plan for *quality text to quality writing* routes through the primary phase and into Key Stage 3. This includes whole-text link reading approaches.

 Build your own knowledge and depth of reading as a school community of ambitious readers grows.

Case study: Building quality text innovation across a trust

Jade Petch, Rachel Hanby, Rebecca Moore and
Holly Howis, Maltby Learning Trust, South Yorkshire

Our multi-academy trust is set within an area of high deprivation in communities that are typically literature poor. Our initial aim when beginning the Opening Doors project was to expose children to a breadth of challenging classic texts, switching them on to the wealth of literature available and breaking down the perception that it is 'not for them'.

When the approach was first broached with teachers, there were preconceptions that the extracts would be inaccessible for 'our children', but the results have been transformative. Along with a strong emphasis on oracy and rehearsal, the strategies have empowered our children to become curious about literature and excited by the opportunities provided by demanding classic texts.

The choice of texts has proven essential to achieving success. In Year 1 at Maltby Manor Academy, 'The Little Land' by Robert Louis Stevenson allowed our children to engage in role play to enhance their understanding and imagination. Drip-feeding Tier 3 vocabulary brought the poetry to life and allowed the children to access the higher level language of the extract and apply it in their learning.

Across our classrooms, we have found that using the Opening Doors illustrations alongside incremental exposure to high-level texts has sparked 'I wonder' questions throughout reading and writing sessions. The use of vivid imagery when studying 'The Door' by Miroslav Holub and 'The Call' by Charlotte Mew enabled Year 6 writers from across the ability range at Maltby Lilly Hall Academy to write with real flair and creativity.

Children were empowered to overcome the learning barriers inherent in complex poetry and prose, which would not have been attempted previously, by revealing slivers of text to them one at a time. This has not only allowed the children to flourish, but also opened doors for our staff to further develop and challenge their thinking.

As teachers became more proficient in applying the 'Opening Doors' approach, we found that their choices became more ambitious. At Ravenfield Primary Academy, children in Year 6 compared and analysed the language choices within a range of historical speeches from Shakespeare and Elizabeth I to Winston Churchill. Archaic language and motivational aspects were carefully unpicked to enable the children to understand the context and meaning. Taster drafts allowed them to manipulate language from across the speeches, sparking their imagination to create motivational battle speeches of their own.

An integral part of the journey from reading to writing was the children having time to dissect these challenging texts and experiment with the complex vocabulary and structures they contained. This helped them to build confidence and understanding and, in turn, apply the forms in their learning independently.

Developing opportunities for our children to build cultural capital is an essential element of learning within Maltby Learning Trust schools. At the heart of our strategy is planning for children to be exposed to their rich literary heritage and to ignite a passion for classic literature. This ambition for excellence has led our English driver group to collaboratively create a canon of literature: a bank of high-quality texts and link reading built around the Opening Doors spine to support and enhance the approach. We are looking forward to continuing our Opening Doors journey to develop a richer English curriculum for all.

The authors would like to thank David Horrigan, executive director of primary education at Maltby Learning Trust, and Heather O'Connor, now the principal at Oasis Academy Henderson Avenue, for their unswerving support for aspirational teaching and learning and our Opening Doors work.

Chapter 5

Principles to Strategies

Leah Crawford

Teachers need to exercise judgement in their contexts and to be flexible in adapting the approach to the needs of their own schools and learners. For that they need a clear understanding of the underlying principles of the approach and they need ownership of the intended outcomes.

Philippa Cordingley and Miranda Bell, *Transferring Learning and Taking Innovation to Scale* (2007)

Imagine this chapter as the pivot point of the book. So far, in the first four chapters, we have explored the core guiding principles of ambitious English provision. Let us pause for a moment, take stock and reflect on those principles: why are they important, and where might we go from here?

Opening doors to ambitious English means:

❧ Striving for excellence with equitable access for all. Chapter 1 explains how this makes sense for reasons of social justice and because all pupils do better when the curriculum is rich and expectations are raised.

❧ Managing inclusive challenge. In Chapter 2, we learnt how supporting learners through challenging texts can accelerate learning and make learning more memorable. Inclusive challenge needs a thoughtful, planned teaching strategy and skilful, live dialogue and decision-making in class.

❧ Teachers selecting rich literary texts and reading them to mine the layers of possibility for teaching. In Chapter 3, we explored how, with rich texts and rich text knowledge, teachers are more likely to be confident in their subject knowledge and take their pupils in creative, purposeful and conceptual directions.

❦ Believing that quality texts create the foundation for reading and writing development. Reading and writing are reciprocal acts of meaning-making. In Chapter 4, we explained that by toggling between the two, we can deepen pupils' cognition and metacognition about the power of the written word.

Why think through our principles?

Why do we need to articulate and acknowledge these shared principles? As the quote from Cordingley and Bell's report for the Centre for the Use of Research and Evidence in Education (CUREE) suggests, these principles are as nothing unless you believe in them and make sense of them through your live practice and in your teaching context. Principles describe an idea; only you can make them a reality through the strategies you adopt and adapt, assessing the impact they have on your children's learning and development.

Principles can also keep you inoculated against approaches in the classroom that might seem efficient and attractive but cause more harm than good in the long term. A recent example of this is the explicit teaching of grammatical structures, which is a strong thread in the Department for Education's *English Programmes of Study: Key Stages 1 and 2* (2013). A seemingly efficient way to deliver all of those grammar objectives is to teach discrete grammar lessons, and many schools took this path in the early days of the 2013 national curriculum. Later on, it became apparent that neither teachers nor pupils were motivated by such lessons, and even if terminology was retained, there was little to no impact on the accuracy or compositional richness of children's writing. If we teach grammar through rich texts and link grammar for reading to the choices we can make as writers, then grammar becomes a fascinating and impactful reading-to-writing strategy.

Here is a great example of writing inspired by James Reeves' poem 'The Hippocrump' (Unit 2 in *Opening Doors to Quality Writing for Ages 6 to 9*). Inspired by Victoria Cox's illustration, Year 3 pupils at Overton Primary in Hampshire first created noun phrases to precisely describe each part of the Hippocrump's body. It is a solid start, but is this challenging enough for Year 3? Dig deeper into the grammar and Reeves' poem opens a series of lines with prepositional phrases in a way that creates dramatic suspense. We wonder what awful or bizarre thing we will learn next about the beast when we get to the end of each line – but we are made to wait because of the grammar! Here are some of the children's taster drafts:

Upon its neck hangs a long, tangled mane.

At the end of each toe is a poisonous claw.

Upon its back are humps, scaly as steel.

Grammar building blocks, taken from Reeves' poem, supported young writers to make fresh choices that create a mix of dramatic humour and fear. The principles of rich texts and reading informing writing keep grammar teaching principled, purposeful and playful.

Communities of teachers as the agents of change

The Opening Doors principles may already align well with your current beliefs, or they may be providing you with new horizons and new directions. The real challenge of teacher professional development is to think hard about how these ideas relate to your existing practice, making decisions about what changes you will make to your teaching repertoire and applying them through cycles of trial and review.

For most of us, this is at best hard and more usually impossible to do well in isolation. In all of the schools where Opening Doors takes root, leaders make available space and resource to build collaborative, critical communities of practice where it is safe to try out new methods, where struggle is supported and where reflection is focused on outcomes, improvement and refinement.

Real development that has an impact on pupils happens when you re-engineer the strategic practice in your school and classroom context.

Repertoires not recipes

The Opening Doors strategies that you will explore in subsequent chapters have proven to be a supportive structure for teachers to enact these principles. They are a flexible toolkit with the aim of building a repertoire and encouraging further innovation, not providing a fixed or linear recipe. It may be helpful to think of the principles as your steadying roots and the strategies as your branches, with potential for further growth.

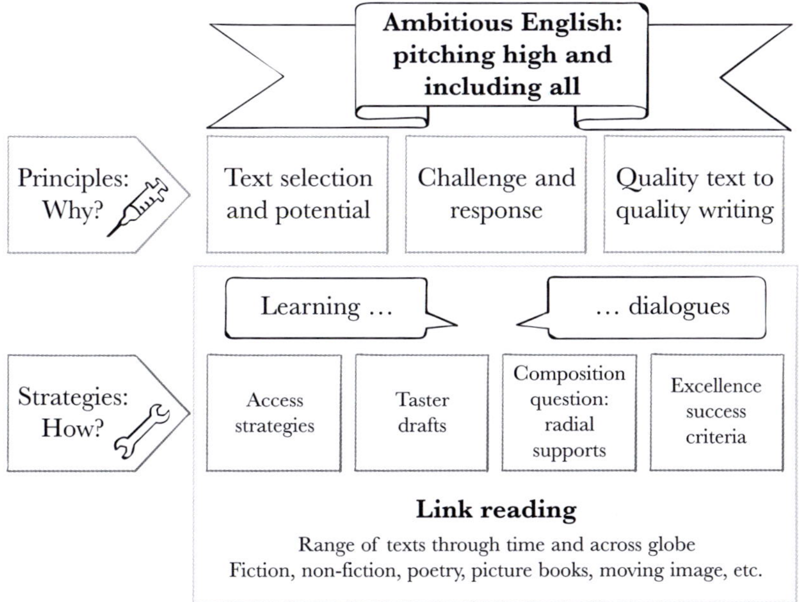

Ambitious English: pitching high and including all

To bring this back to the classroom, let us walk through two scenarios for using the deeply challenging sonnet by the radical Romantic poet Percy Bysshe Shelley entitled 'Ozymandias' – the Greek name for the pharaoh Ramses II:

I met a traveller from an antique land,

Who said – 'Two vast and trunkless legs of stone

Stand in the desert. … Near them, on the sand,

Half sunk a shattered visage lies, whose frown,

And wrinkled lip, and sneer of cold command,

Tell that its sculptor well those passions read

Which yet survive, stamped on these lifeless things,

The hand that mocked them, and the heart that fed;

And on the pedestal, these words appear:

My name is Ozymandias, King of Kings;

Look on my Works, ye Mighty, and despair!

Nothing beside remains. Round the decay

Of that colossal Wreck, boundless and bare

The lone and level sands stretch far away.'

Lynsey is a talented Year 4 leader and teacher at All Saints Junior School in Hampshire. She has designed a history-based learning journey based on the Egyptians that will explore the rise and fall of this ancient civilisation.

She thinks that the central image in 'Ozymandias', the decaying statue of an autocratic ruler abandoned in the desert, will be fascinating to her class, and will support her to teach the concept of the transitory power of rulers and compare this to the power of poetry. Can she use adaptive strategies to render the symbol and satire in this poem accessible to her 8- and 9-year-olds?

Without deep understanding, Lynsey might share an image of the statue that now sits in the British Museum, explore some of the difficult vocabulary to improve access, reveal the poem and then ask a big Opening Doors question like, 'How does the poem affect your view of the ruler Ozymandias?' She might think that this ticks the boxes of access with challenge, built on the concept of symbolism. I imagine you would agree that this sequence might work with 13- or 14-year-olds, but it is unlikely to create sufficiently deep engagement and meaning-making in Year 4.

Let us look at what actually played out in Lynsey's classroom:

- ❦ The class responded to a commonly used artists' recreation of the crumbling statue, available online.

- ❦ Words and phrases from the poem were introduced and their meanings explored. Lynsey asked her pupils: 'Can you link any words to parts of the image and explain why you have linked them?' and 'Are there words that present a different view to the image?'

- Lynsey explained the context of the poem's creation: the English poet Shelley hears that the remains of a great statue of Ramses II are about to be brought to England and he has been challenged to write a poem about it. The class then used the image and slivers of language to write their own description of the statue: what would a poet say about it? They discussed similarities and differences in their viewpoints as poets.

- Rather than reveal the whole poem, Lynsey structured a strategic slow reveal that gave her class the time and space to build the traveller's view of the statue from the description, then compared this to the words on the pedestal – 'Look on my Works, ye Mighty and despair!' – and discussed what they thought Ramses wanted people to feel about him when they looked at the statue.

- Finally, they compared this to the view they have as readers of the statue – and of Ramses – in the final three lines of the poem. The class then metacognitively tracked how their view of the statue had changed throughout the lesson and what in the poem had led them to change their view.

- Quite wonderfully, the class visited the British Museum the very next week where the statue – only imagined by Shelley when writing the poem – is now displayed. It is available at: https://www.britishmuseum.org/collection/object/Y_EA19.

- Back in class, Lynsey asked the pupils to recall how the poem had made them feel about the statue compared to their feelings about the statue in the museum.

- The whole class then grappled with this masterstroke of a question: 'Which do you think is more powerful: Ramses II, his statue or the poem?'

Here are some of the Year 4 written responses:

I think the view of Ramses in the poem is most powerful because it says 'My name is Ozymandias King of Kings look on my works ye mighty and despair!' This has the power to make me feel unsafe and worried because he is controlling and it sounds like he's here with us. I don't think Ramses/

Ozymandias is powerful. All his power has gone into the poem, which says his power has been almost completely forgotten!

The poem is most powerful because it still has the power to change my emotions. The pharaoh is dead and has no power over anyone.

Of course, there are so many more layers of understanding to build from this poem: the notion of the sonnet form and its argument structure and the notion of revolutionary politics in Romanticism, to name but two. However, with judicious teaching approaches these young readers have developed their ideas about how structure links to effect, how poems can change our view of things and most importantly, perhaps, they have begun to think about how art outlives us all, if it has the power to speak across generations.

A journey through the extended metaphor of Old King Time in Eliza Cook's 'Song of Old Time' (Unit 7 in *Opening Doors to a Richer English Curriculum for Ages 10 to 13*) would be a generative link text to 'Ozymandias', comparing the sands of time to the 'lone and level sands' in Shelley's final line. Thematic links to fate, time and power could be made with Philip Pullman's novella *Clockwork*, Valerie Bloom's poem 'Time' and John Agard's 'Clockwise'.

Link reading

Naturally, all 80 units are built on Opening Doors principles, but if you would specifically like more ideas for units on the passage of time and the power of poetry, try:

- 'Mementos' by Charlotte Brontë (Unit 9 in *Opening Doors to Quality Writing for Ages 10 to 13*)

- 'Blue Remembered Hills' by A. E. Housman (Unit 14 in *Opening Doors to Quality Writing for Ages 10 to 13*)

- 'Leisure' by W. H. Davies (Unit 2 in *Opening Doors to a Richer English Curriculum for Ages 6 to 9*)

- 'Dear March – Come In –' by Emily Dickinson (Unit 4 in *Opening Doors to a Richer English Curriculum for Ages 6 to 9*)

❧ 'The Song of Wandering Aengus' by W. B. Yeats (Unit 3 in *Opening Doors to a Richer English Curriculum for Ages 10 to 13*)

If you would like to explore units that integrate the teaching of grammar with effect and compositional choices, try:

❧ 'The Hippocrump' by James Reeves (Unit 2 in *Opening Doors to Quality Writing for Ages 6 to 9*)

❧ 'Slowly' by James Reeves (Unit 3 in *Opening Doors to Quality Writing for Ages 6 to 9*)

❧ 'Hurt No Living Thing' by Christina Rossetti (Unit 3 in *Opening Doors to a Richer English Curriculum for Ages 6 to 9*)

❧ 'Cat!' by Eleanor Farjeon (Unit 7 in *Opening Doors to a Richer English Curriculum for Ages 6 to 9*)

❧ 'Sympathy' by Paul Laurence Dunbar (Unit 5 in *Opening Doors to a Richer English Curriculum for Ages 10 to 13*)

❧ 'Speak of the North!' by Charlotte Brontë (Unit 2 in *Opening Doors to a Richer English Curriculum for Ages 10 to 13*)

Key points on moving from principles to strategies

Think critically with others about your principles – about the extent to which your current knowledge, beliefs and practice are aligned with providing excellence with equity.

Commit to extending your familiarity with and knowledge of rich texts from across time and across the globe. The suite of five 'Opening Doors' books with their central and linked texts provide a rich starting point.

Think, plan, trial and reflect on adaptations to teaching in a safe and critical professional community, whether this is in your school, cluster, multi-academy trust or a supportive online community.

Assess what works by paying close attention to changes in pupil outcomes – behaviours, motivation and confidence as well as spoken and written outcomes. Guidance from research is just guidance.

Case study: A finessed reading provision

Louise Trim, Hordle Church of England Primary School, Lymington, Hampshire

It has always been my firm belief that what you read determines the writer you become. It was on this principle that our English curriculum was built, with rich text choices at the very heart.

Curriculum design

We mapped out our children's reading journey, ensuring there were opportunities to read a wide range of genres and themes and to celebrate significant authors and poets. Next, we developed a rationale for each book, so the whole staff team understood the justification for studying specific texts. For instance, *The Iron Man* by Ted Hughes wasn't there just because it is a classic science fiction novel; we had chosen to study this story because of the vivid imagery, the poetic use of rhythm and sound effects, and the contrast between fear and humour. The same depth of rationale applies to the texts we choose for reception as much as for Year 6.

Developing critical thinkers

Having explored the big questions from Opening Doors, and having also been on a journey with the Let's Think in English programme, it was clear that we wanted to find a way to further challenge our children to think deeply about text concepts, like structure, symbolism and form. As a result, we created a progression document with examples of question stems for critical and evaluative thinking.

We know that conceptual thinking can only build if children make links across and between texts, so when we approach a new unit, we will think about opportunities to bridge from one text to another. For instance, we recently spent one day immersed in *The Great Kapok Tree* by Lynne Cherry. This is not a challenging text per se – its fable-like message is a great springboard to a conservation unit – so we know it is important to use a challenging question. We asked, 'Is this a believable story?' The aim was to challenge the children conceptually, encouraging them to make links to genre and purpose.

Next, we revealed a letter from the author, which reveals that 30 years after publishing her book, the situation in the rainforest has only worsened. Her hopeful, fable-like ending has not come to pass. Over the following days, we studied speeches by Greta Thunberg and Severn Cullis-Suzuki from the book *Talking History* (Haig and Lennon, 2022), looking at the ways that rhetorical devices can be used judiciously to present a powerful message. The children had never been more motivated to write:

I am here today to be the voice for the voiceless, for the countless animals dying across our planet. Our earth is dying because of you. I urge you to stop killing our rainforests. If you don't, there could be frightful consequences.

Murron Smith (aged 7)

The role of Opening Doors

Opening Doors has been important because of its teaching principles and how it enables principled CPD. Using the units from the books as a foundation, teachers have been able to identify a range of different strategies for each phase of a learning journey. One of our most successful INSET days was working in teams to take an Opening Doors unit and work collaboratively to think about how we could further develop the ideas and adapt it to provide inclusive challenge. At the end of the day, each team articulated what kinds of adaptations they had made and what the biggest shifts in their teaching were going to be to capture metacognitively their intent and the journey ahead.

There is no question that teachers at Hordle now feel more confident about planning for more challenging texts – the why and the how.

Part 2

Key Opening Doors Strategies

ReSource 10

Chapter 6
Link Reading

Bob Cox

Learning involves making meaning from what we remember … But one reason teaching is such a complex and absorbing profession is because this isn't enough: we also have to help our students understand what they've learned and make meaningful connections between ideas.

Niki Kaiser, 'Meaningful Memory' (2020)

Many of you reading this – but probably not all of you – will have been avid book lovers since you were young. Maybe you were surrounded by stories, poems and drama at home; perhaps a teacher introduced you to a gripping tale; perhaps the inspiration of a library or librarian played a big part. For some, formal GCSE set text immersion could have been memorable; for others, it may have been a switch-off. However, if reading becomes an enjoyable habit, it is a gift for life.

Professor Teresa Cremin has led a hugely influential and successful initiative in recent years emphasising teachers as readers and setting up reading groups across the UK focusing on reading for pleasure. She reminds us, in research-led ways, that children are more likely to develop into lifelong readers when they are supported by teachers who read regularly and talk about books themselves.[1]

Sadly, throughout my career, there has been a huge issue with reluctant readers and those whose literacy levels dip as they get older. Not everyone takes to reading easily and not everyone shares the delight of stories instantly. The consequences of low literacy levels can be

---

1   See https://ourfp.org.

stark. The National Literacy Trust's review into literacy and life expectancy includes some disturbing findings:

> The national gap in life expectancy between children from communities with the highest and lowest vulnerability to literacy problems in the country is staggering:
>
> ❧ A boy growing up in a ward with one of the highest vulnerabilities to literacy problems in the country has a life expectancy *26.1 years shorter* than a boy growing up in a ward with one of the lowest vulnerabilities to literacy problems.
>
> ❧ A girl growing up in a ward with one of the highest vulnerabilities to literacy problems in the country has a life expectancy *20.9 years shorter* than a girl growing up in a ward with one of the lowest vulnerabilities to literacy problems. (Gilbert et al., 2018: 5)

More recently, a report from the Institute of Fiscal Studies (Farquharson et al., 2022a) has outlined the continuing disadvantage gap in the UK. One of the authors, economist Imran Tahir, observes: 'Among pupils who are behind expectations at the end of primary school, fewer than one in ten goes on to earn good GCSEs in English and maths – meaning that we bake in failure from an early age' (Farquharson et al., 2022b).

It isn't our role in this book to go into a lengthy discussion about the reasons for this, but we do know that under-resourced schools are full of teachers hungry for equity and excellence for their pupils, and we believe that having high expectations for every child's reading diet is vital. Why should anyone miss out?

We see many of our schools working at the root of the problem, nurturing teachers with the skills and knowledge to make interventions count and making rich reading material the entitlement of every pupil. Quality teachers have a way of assessing need and diversifying to intervene with issues of basic literacy as well as aspirational goals.

It really is possible for primary pupils who find literacy hard to remain part of challenging whole-class reading. We call the systems we have worked on with schools 'link reading', which has at its heart flexibility, choice and coherence. Connections are made across texts, creating schemas in the mind around which learning can stick. Challenging reading therefore becomes the hub of the curriculum, whereas 'wider reading' has always seemed to infer an option or a final extension when all else is completed.

So, how can link reading provide a rich foundation for all learners?

Using concepts

If you are teaching an aspect of English, then a range of whole-text reading can be linked to that concept. For example, if your core text has the potential for you to teach effective personification, then you can assemble a range of whole-text link reading to support that aim. Teaching a concept rather than 'doing' a poem or book gives English dynamism and purpose.

Zoom in for depth, detail and specific teaching (as in Chapter 3 on text choice and concepts), but go broader with selections that form schemas and enable the mind to sort, sift, compare, contrast and, of course, remember. In this way, the power of the learning via the core text is deepened and widened by pupils finding appropriate link reading on the same concept. This is a route-way to coherence as well as inclusion.

Providing access to equity and excellence

A common concept can support a web of interlinked reading recommendations, enabling access for all pupils by including diverse texts with a range of complexity. Pupil options should always be paramount, but participation is a non-negotiable – they cannot opt out of reading altogether.

Teachers are talented at suggesting new texts, helping pupils to find novel directions and working with the school's greatest literary resource – the librarian. Here is one example of how a librarian can provide support with the logistical issues that arise when planning link reading selections:

1. The teacher and librarian make link reading selections together based around a specific concept or theme.

2. The link reading texts are organised in the library according to the concept or theme.

3. The texts are transferred to the classroom as a satellite of the library for the pre-planned unit.

Choosing a range and diversity of texts

Typically, you might include picture books and modern children's literature from around the globe along with snippets from classics to form an eclectic mix of quality texts. They should all demonstrate the chosen concept, giving you the chance to integrate reading and insights from any of the chosen texts into your teaching and discussions. Teachers don't reach for challenging texts in an ad hoc way; rather, they know that progression and sequencing are part of a big map of learning in their school.

Enhancing curriculum coherence

Schools need to allow sufficient curriculum time for the reading to commence and then accelerate, all the while eliciting questions and responses. That is the nature of English: it knows no boundaries, as long as the text has depth. Creating coherence via concepts enables you to link priorities to your overall curriculum design.

Many schools bring the link reading selections (which could be 20 or 30 texts) out of the library and into the classroom to demonstrate that link reading is part of the high expectations for the lesson. Teachers then facilitate the process by guiding personal choices and emphasising connections across the concepts. When reluctant readers see everyone else revelling in the available literature, they are more likely to want to join in!

Of course, teachers can't read all the link reading selections themselves, which is why partnerships across staff, librarians, external experts and the school community are so vital in a thriving school. I can recall exciting English changes being jumpstarted by a budget commitment to the library and the fun of selecting books together around concepts or themes. When I revisit our Opening Doors schools, teachers tell me they feel more confident and well-read, and because of the increased metacognitive talk and staffroom banter about new quality texts.

Long-term impact

Here is an example of how link reading can be planned for as part of a rationale for English rather than as a discrete or occasional activity.

Let us suppose you are teaching effective personification using Paul Laurence Dunbar's 'The Wind and the Sea' (and to enjoy a poem written in 1896!): https://www.poetry.com/poem/28963/the-wind-and-the-sea.

This is the core text; you might use the whole poem with older children or a few lines with younger ones, but be flexible. Using a few lines and going deeper is growing in popularity in our schools. Whatever their age, a sliver of a quality text can support the children's journey to quality writing with rigour and enjoyment.

The lines below can be treated as a core text through which you plan detailed language study, as in the 'Adlestrop' example (Chapter 13) or Sue Hardy-Dawson's 'Fog Warning' (Chapter 4), with a focus on the personality given to the wind and sea. Afterwards, the link reading will set up a quality reading culture to deepen the experiences you have signposted in the focused teaching. Meanwhile, the pupils' knowledge about different aspects of personification will grow.

The wind was young and the sea was old,
But their cries went up together;
The wind was warm and the sea was cold,
For age makes wintry weather.
So they cried aloud and they wept amain,
Till the sky grew dark to hear it;
And out of its folds crept the misty rain,
In its shroud, like a troubled spirit.

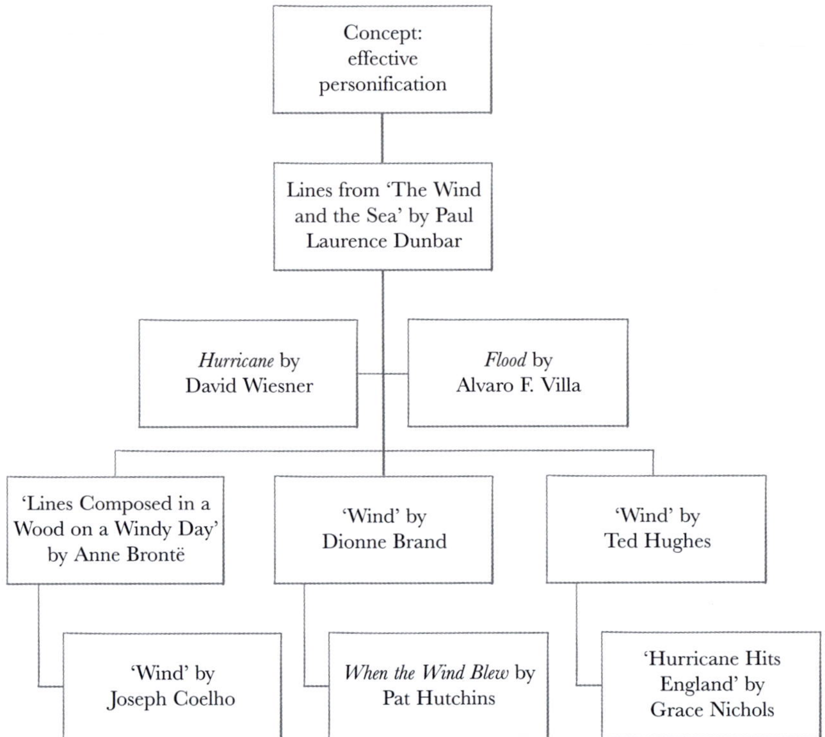

Link reading on the concept of personification

The figure above demonstrates how the core text (Dunbar) can link with recommended reading on a similar theme as well as with the teaching of personification. This is a powerful approach which enables connections to be made across multiple texts. As a result, link reading comes to occupy a central place in the curriculum, and literary journeys from Brontë to Coelho are ranged before your pupils' minds like a feast! I have deliberately included a huge readability range in this example to show the potential of link reading, but teachers can, of course, select texts appropriate to their pupils.

This strategy merges highly focused direct teaching, where all kinds of language study are possible (e.g. line layout, metaphor, exploring new vocabulary), with a breadth of reading and plenty of choice for all. A wide range of connections can be made with the wind, the poet's voice and personification. The accompanying illustration can support initial links by forming a bridge between the power expressed in Dunbar's poem and ideas about other personifications that could be invented by the children.

As a routine part of the English curriculum, a diet of link reading can provide teachers with opportunities to repeat concepts (such as personification) but applied across different texts and with a huge range of choice built in. In her post 'Meaningful Memory', Niki Kaiser (2020) from the Norwich Research School highlights very clearly the importance of both memory and meaning. A policy of link reading gives pupils the chance to make such meaning every day in the classroom.

To keep connections and associations alive, the children can be recommended texts which present them with new reading challenges. For some, it might be Pat Hutchins' *When the Wind Blew*, whilst others might be ready to experience the imagination of Anne Brontë. Routes to inclusion and excellence should be signposted daily via all the learning dialogues which will illuminate new ideas from such challenging texts. Classroom discussions about personification could come from any one of the texts in the figure on page 70. Pupils will start to understand link reading as a system – and will soon demand it!

Opportunities to read at home can be enhanced and then followed up and enriched in the classroom. Try the following ideas:

- Sticky notes posted by every pupil every few days including favourite sections, quotes or descriptions.

- Pupils create tables listing examples of personification linked across texts.

- The teacher intervenes to introduce new examples.

- Displays and recitals to deepen learning.

- Talk, talk, talk!

I would not advise one book review after another or anything that will become a routine. The texts will be different, so focus on short, snappy exercises that involve talking through examples to maintain the buzz. This will also give you the chance to interject with teaching points. The link reading shouldn't become a separate activity from the curriculum or be seen as optional. Status matters; quality reading as the centre of school life sounds brilliant to me!

Link reading is about pupils being immersed in ambitious reading, not in one classroom but across the whole school. Every child is entitled to new reading experiences, so planning for it offers systems within which this aspiration is normalised. Ambition is relative to each child, so Wiesner's *Hurricane* will represent progress for some, whilst others may be ready to tackle Ted Hughes. How challenging *Hurricane* becomes is then dependent on the questions you ask and the inferences the pupils make, so once again the role of the teacher is paramount.

You can take a look at some of the examples of pupils' work inspired by Dionne Brand's 'Wind' on the Crown House Publishing website: https://www.crownhouse.co.uk/featured-opening-doors-to-a-richer-english-curriculum-pupils-work-ages-6-9-ins1. The poem features in Unit 1 in *Opening Doors to a Richer English Curriculum for Ages 6 to 9*.

Planning and expectations

Imagine the power of link reading embedded throughout the primary phase. By the end of Year 6, the pupils will be confident readers with broad experience of a range of literary styles and language. Those whose literacy levels were lower will have received suitable texts appropriate to their reading age, but always within a context of challenge and new learning.

Inclusion means access for all and appropriate reading progress for all too. Every pupil is learning and every pupil is experiencing interventions and suggestions. Support provided by teaching assistants, reading volunteers, teachers and parents will ensure constant monitoring. Guided groups can be formed for specific needs when necessary, but without overt labelling so the groups can evolve according to need. The pitch is high, but the scaffolding is constant!

Making a difference

Think about any book or poem you now love which you would never have attempted without a teacher's knowledge and encouragement. The role of the teacher has always been to take pupils to places they can't reach by themselves. It is potentially life-changing.

Linking in quality reading and progressively building it through the curriculum can be very exciting, although it requires determination and must be vigorously pursued. When done well, your pupils will take a richer reading history to secondary school along with higher levels of confidence. Fewer pupils should feel disaffected or nervous about English, and advanced pupils will have experienced a richer diet with more creative connections. Consequently, they will be much better equipped for the literary demands of the secondary curriculum than they would following narrow test-led preparations.

Ambition and inclusion can and should be bedfellows, with immersion in stories and poems central to any school's reading policy. As Sir Michael Morpurgo said in his 2016 lecture to the Book Trust: 'Children have to want to learn. So give them the love of story first, the rest will follow.'

You will find link reading suggestions in all the 'Opening Doors' books, although the idea has been developed with more coherence in *Opening Doors to a Richer English Curriculum for Ages 6 to 9* and *Opening Doors to a Richer English Curriculum for Ages 10 to 13*. As the book series has grown, and as I have travelled to hundreds of schools, I have come to appreciate the dynamic effect of high expectations for quality reading and the central role of the teacher. From initially just recommending a reading list, the concept of linking in reading as a key part of the curriculum has developed. Please ask for a visit to one of our schools to see how reading ambition can be applied!

Key points on link reading

Link reading can emphasise high expectations. It is a truth universally acknowledged (Jane Austen, of course!) that pupils will do what their teachers *expect*. Being realistically ambitious is part of the role of educators, so prioritise a culture for exciting reading journeys.

Linking can connect thinking around a concept:

- Link the choice of texts to a concept for the teaching of English.

- Plan for a large range of texts with suitable choices for all learners.

- Examples of a concept in various texts can be used to link and connect learning in class.

Link texts can be chosen and explored partly in curriculum time:

- Ensure curriculum time is set aside for silent reading as well as for discussions/teaching.

- Sticky notes on display boards could record pupil comments on a previous night's reading at home.

- Texts can be brought into the classroom from the library to *facilitate questions* about character, theme, setting or the chosen concept (e.g. personification).

Planning for link reading. A strategic action plan is needed to ensure link reading choices becomes a whole-school policy. For example, a Year 4 teacher must know what the reading curriculum was for Year 3 and what it will be for Year 5.

Link reading has *funding* implications, of course. Part of the action plan will be funding for link reading texts to be provided via the library and then using classrooms as satellites, with texts continually borrowed and returned.

Link reading strategies require a wide search for quality texts. You will find useful support for *choosing the texts* themselves via the 'Opening Doors' series, the Centre for Literacy in Primary Education (CLPE) and the National Literacy Trust.

Case study: Link reading journeys

Kerrie Hope, Ryefield Primary School, Uxbridge[2]

Each half term, our Opening Doors text is the springboard into a scheme of work devised around a modern author. The ambitious, high-quality extract literally opens the door to the objectives

---

2   You may also be interested in reading Kerrie's article for the NATE magazine *Primary Matters* about developing the English curriculum (Hope, 2021).

of the reading and writing journey. The link reading rationale is carried into our shared and guided reading sessions, in which children are exposed to an extensive range of companion texts. By increasing the children's reading mileage, we have awoken their appetites for making connections between texts, themselves and the world around them. They are reading for meaning.

More importantly, the links don't stop at a thematic premise, as link reading has opened our thinking to source texts that focus on authorial technique. For example, with our Year 5 'scientists and explorers' theme, the fiction and poetry across the term is selected in order to analyse the concept of tension and suspense. Consequently, our teaching illuminates how an author can manipulate a reader through language choices and sentence structure.

In class, I have found that a habit of ambitious reading experiences can stimulate the voice of every child. Previously, I limited the reading choices so my struggling readers and writers were not overwhelmed, and, to be honest, I only selected texts that were in my own comfort zone. By changing my mindset, I have inspired and enthused all of the personalities and abilities in my classroom. Plus, over time, I have seen that exploring eminent authors' voices has opened a torrent of independent thought from my burgeoning writers. I can hear echoes of the texts we have read in their work and each piece has its own style.

The impact on the children at Ryefield is that they are far exceeding our previous expectations, and they are writing with strong, individual voices. Link reading has sparked in them the confidence to trust in their own creative instincts. They are attentive in their reading and enjoy spotting parallels between texts, whilst actively searching for ideas and techniques to help them become better writers. Their reading and writing has pleasure and purpose at its core.

Resource 12

Chapter 7

Taster Drafts: Writing for Reading

Bob Cox

An understanding of meaning isn't arrived at straightaway and all at once. It is discovered, negotiated, made, arrived at organically.

Aidan Chambers, *Tell Me: Children, Reading and Talk*
(2011)

There is nothing new in short-burst writing, but our schools have utilised it in particularly ambitious ways. Time limited and/or word limited taster drafts can be a major way of lifting writing standards when used as part of quality text to quality writing journeys. One answer I give to the conundrum of how to improve writing is universal: writing develops with practice and routines, but the routines must be challenging, varied and regular. It isn't possible to become a better writer without doing lots of writing.

The taster draft can be the vehicle for your pupils' daily energetic expressions of imitations, experiments and quirky possibilities, which should always be stimulated by a range of literary styles and new vocabulary. Taster draft writing can therefore make a significant contribution to the organic process of learning articulated above by Aidan Chambers. We often see teachers setting short-burst writing well before the full text has been revealed.

Taster drafts can be stimulated by an initial introduction to a text and the author's style. They should come quickly in the reading-to-writing process as a springboard for enthusiasm and a chance to apply ideas. In my extensive coaching and observation work, I have sometimes noticed that pupils are set a lot of exercises that preclude any writing at all until the end of the unit when a summative title is set or a regular test takes place. Pupils have also told me that they 'only write on a Friday' or 'only when they are taken to the hall'. Pupils latch on to when the writing seems to 'matter'. We want it to matter every day!

How can the writing process be developed for maximum motivation?

Writing can be at the centre of the curriculum on a daily basis and integrated coherently alongside speaking, listening and reading. For years, reading and analysing have been used to stimulate writing but writing for reading is just as vital. Doug Lemov et al. state in *Reading Reconsidered* (2016: 204): 'The better students write, the better they'll read. More specifically, the more intentional writing practice students get, the more tuned in they'll be to the choices authors make.'

Imitating an author's style and making some early attempts to experiment with a concept can significantly support children's routes to comprehension. Tasters can also provide a focused vehicle for assessment for learning, enabling the teacher to teach to need and devise writing processes that enable the children to aspire towards a sustained and summative piece. Please browse through the many examples of pupils' work (both work in progress and sustained pieces) on the Crown House Publishing website: https://www.crownhouse.co.uk/bob-cox. Just click on each book to find the relevant links.

Pupils should experience a lot of enjoyment on their creative journey. Tasters should be time limited or word limited, with every pupil potentially giving feedback, attention levels remaining high and expert knowledge being offered at the right time – just when their enthusiasm for the text is at its highest. Our schools have found that a focus on tasters early in the unit has enabled pupils to memorise and begin to understand key concepts without being flooded with too many ideas at once. Simultaneously, advanced learners are also challenged because of the richness of the text and the deep scope for learning that it presents.

The potential for excellence is introduced stage by stage, with all pupils finding their way through the challenge of a text. Some teachers set additional drafts to ask pupils to go deeper, and they often use one of the linked texts to inspire more interesting work.

Writing to a word limit can be emphasised as a polished discipline in itself. There is nothing like it to convey that every word counts for its meaning and contribution. An excellent book to spur your thinking on the teaching of writing is *On the Write Track* by James Clements (2023).

How can the taster draft support equity and excellence?

The taster draft fires up the learning as the children's familiarisation with the text style deepens. Dr Megan Mansworth (2021: 41) writes that 'the beauty of teaching to the top well is that we are able to introduce students to challenging concepts, ideas and knowledge that will also simplify their future learning'.

The best way to explain the rich potential in tasters is via an example. Let us imagine you have focused a core concept for new knowledge and learning around this extract from *October, October* by Katya Balen (2020: 7), winner of the 2022 Yoto Carnegie Medal:

We live in the woods and we are wild.

Tonight we howl at the star-dusted sky. We throw our voices and shape them and mix them and mould them like clay. We can stretch our sounds so that they reach the very tops of our tallest trees and down to the secret-filled earth and so that they tangle in the brambles and skim across the pond because this world is ours and we are alone.

Just us.

A pocket of people in a pocket of a world that's small as a marble. We are tiny and we are everything and we are wild.

We live in the woods.

We live in the woods and we are wild.

As we explored in Chapter 4 on quality text to quality writing, the hub of your ambitious English teaching should revolve around the scope of the text. Reflecting on this beautiful prose with a reading for teaching eye,[1] it is apparent that there is the potential for learning about the concept of describing epic landscapes. Long sentences deliberately use the conjunction 'and' with hyphenated, inflated phrases, such as 'secret-filled earth' and 'star-dusted sky', all echoing the wild impression. It is a startling passage, close to the beginning of the story, and contrasts the grand feel of nature with the revelation of the 'pocket' image that shrinks everything into a marble.

You could start with the illustration by Victoria Cox. This sentence could accompany it before you reveal the whole extract: 'A pocket of people in a pocket of a world that's small as a marble. We are tiny and we are everything and we are wild.' Ask the children:

❧ What images can you identify in the marble?

❧ What might the marble represent?

❧ What other descriptions could you write which would belong in a passage about people who are 'tiny' and 'everything'?

The final question would take your pupils into a brief taster draft and the beginnings of imitation. Then, the revealing of the full passage becomes an absolute fascination.

There are many other creative possibilities, such as starting with the image of the wild woods. Or you might choose to focus on deep objectives – for example:

❧ How well can you explain how the author creates an epic feel to this passage?

❧ How well can you write about an epic, grand statement around an emotion or setting?

You can find link reading on describing epic landscapes, both poetry and prose, to initiate connections, strengthen schemas and broaden understanding of language and style in Chapter 6. However, here are two contrasting suggestions:

❧ 'I, Too' by Langston Hughes: https://poets.org/poem/i-too

❧ 'Morte d'Arthur' by Alfred, Lord Tennyson: https://www.poetryfoundation.org/poems/45370/morte-darthur

---

1 Reading for teaching is the phrase I use to describe the way we assess a text for its potential for learning.

The beginning of the epic narrative poem 'Morte d'Arthur' is very famous and is well worth looking up:

So all day long the noise of battle roll'd

Among the mountains by the winter sea;

Until King Arthur's table, man by man,

Had fallen in Lyonnesse about their Lord,

Taster drafts work best when you explore key points of language and show how the author has, in this instance, created an epic feel, and then ask the pupils to write a draft which demonstrates a flavour of the author's style.

For Katya Balen's *October, October*, the process might go something like this:

1. Learning from text:

    *   Explore other examples of epic descriptions in *October, October*.

    *   Demonstrate how the prosody in a line like 'Tonight we howl at the star-dusted sky' reflects the meaning.[2]

    *   Emphasise the 't' at the start and end of 'tonight' and contrast the sharpness with the drawn-out vowel sound in 'howl', which gives the listener an echo of the wild. The hyphenated 'star-dusted' introduces a figurative connotation into the image and makes links in the mind with dreams, possibilities, fantasy and a vast universe of openness.

    *   Look at the use of contrasts in the extract.

    *   Consider the use of repetition.

    *   The meaning is in the reading so read it aloud and share many times.

    *   Taste some of the link reading suggestions, even as snippets.

---

2 Prosody refers to the patterns and rhythms in the text – a kind of music made by the sounds and intonation – all of which enforce the meaning.

2.   Taster draft application:

Use Katya Balen's description and what you have learnt from it to write no more than 75 words on one of the following:

❦   Start your draft with: 'We are tiny and we are everything and we are wild …' Tell the reader more about being tiny.

❦   Describe a setting in a world of pocket people as small as a marble. Remember that the world will have epic dimensions from their perspective!

❦   Choose any place or atmosphere that you can describe in a grand, epic way.

❦   Try a mini saga of 50 words. (This would be a perfect vehicle for imitating the epic feel of the passage and creating the sense of a complete world. Find out more about the mini saga form in Lindsay Clandfield's (2002) article.)

It is a huge joy to feel the silence in the room and sense the children's brains whirring, but this will only happen if you have set up the learning well by highlighting Balen's superb rhythmic writing. Repeat readings from you, with sections echoed by the pupils, will embed the meaning and complement your vocabulary explorations.

The taster drafts are stepping stones towards sustained writing, so ensure that every draft is kept carefully in books as evidence of progress and to show how resilience can grow through advice and toil.

Taster drafts should be introduced as early as possible at the primary phase. We know of schools using Christina Rossetti's poetry at Key Stage 1 (see both of the 'Opening Doors' books for ages 6 to 9), or try a picture book like *A House That Once Was* by Julie Fogliano to stimulate writing for reading at an early stage in the process.

Teachers have found the following example – a sliver of text from *Pinocchio* by Carlo Collodi (Unit 13 in *Opening Doors to a Richer English Curriculum for Ages 6 to 9*) – to be particularly inspiring. This is the scene where Pinocchio is still a piece of wood and is speaking to the carpenter, Master Cherry:

He turned his terrified eyes all around the room to try and discover where the little voice could possibly have come from, but he saw nobody! He looked under the bench – nobody; he looked into a cupboard that was always shut – nobody; he looked into a basket of shavings and sawdust – nobody; he even opened the door of the shop and gave a glance into the street – and still nobody. Who, then, could it be?

Sara Abbas, English lead, has led pioneering work at Mulgrave Primary School. For example, read below how a Year 3 pupil responded to the passage:

In my opinion, I think he is annoyed, because he heard a strange voice and the character couldn't find where it came from. The evidence to support the text is: 'he even opened the door of the shop and gave a glance into the street!'

I noticed that the text is written in the present tense, from the perspective of the character: the text is full of effective verbs such as 'he looked' and 'he opened'.

Additionally, the text is also full of prepositions such as 'around'. This tells me that the character is desperate to search for the truth and there is a sense of urgency, but also distraction.

Catalina (Year 3, Mulgrave Primary School)

The teacher very intelligently linked *Pinocchio* with *The Miraculous Journey of Edward Tulane* by Kate DiCamillo, which resulted in the following draft by the same pupil showing the learning and connections she had made:

Edward sank, sank, sank towards the blue vast sea-endless; he fell deep, deep, deep until he hit the hard, rocky surface-endless. He tumbled tremendously and flapped his arms desperately trying to pick himself up - endless; he had no choice but to look up until he saw a light up above in the sea. His eyes were painted on, so he couldn't close his eyes.

In an ambitious curriculum, whole-text reading should be an expectation that is woven into the everyday richness of English. The key writing processes delivered through taster drafts can be inspired by link texts as well as the core extract.

Link reading

❦ *Pinocchio* by Carlo Collodi

❦ *The Miraculous Journey of Edward Tulane* by Kate DiCamillo

❦ *Boy in the Tower* by Polly Ho-Yen

❦ 'I, Too' by Langston Hughes

❦ *The Island at the End of Everything* by Kiran Millwood Hargrave

❦ *The Wolf Wilder* by Katherine Rundell

❦ 'Morte D'Arthur' by Alfred, Lord Tennyson

The following units from the 'Opening Doors' books should also support some inspiration around epic descriptions:

❦ 'Hurt No Living Thing' by Christina Rossetti (Unit 3 in *Opening Doors to a Richer English Curriculum for Ages 6 to 9*)

❦ 'Over the Hills and Far Away' by Hilary McKay and 'Blackberry Blue' by Jamila Gavin (Unit 8 in *Opening Doors to a Richer English Curriculum for Ages 6 to 9*)

❦ 'Speak of the North!' by Charlotte Brontë (Unit 2 in *Opening Doors to a Richer English Curriculum for Ages 10 to 13*)

❦ 'The Door in the Wall' by H. G. Wells (Unit 10 in *Opening Doors to a Richer English Curriculum for Ages 10 to 13*)

Key points on taster drafts

Tasting means the start of *demonstrating* learning by writing freely:

- Tasks can imitate the style of the author.
- Tasks can demonstrate some understanding of the concept.
- Tasks can show the beginnings of new knowledge being applied.

Tasting is *brief*:

- Keep it time limited or word limited.
- Every child should be able to respond well; advanced learners can show sophistication.
- Thinking engines and group talk can support the process, but writing in silence should then follow.

Tasting supports *assessment for learning*:

- The feeding back of the taster draft in classroom dialogues should be linked with suggestions for improvement from you as the teacher. Some peer assessment could be effective too but your knowledgeable steering is essential.
- Feedback can be advice to the whole class as well as individuals.
- Ask yourself how effective the writing has been in practising the deeper objective.
- Ask yourself if an understanding of the concept is growing.

Tasting is *writing for reading*:

❦ The writing experiences afforded by a taster draft can build a rich repertoire over time and throughout the curriculum. Writing to a set aspect of English can develop the confidence pupils need to read and explore the full text with confidence and understand the meaning.

Tasting can *build* towards the main meal:

❦ Set tasters according to your judgement as to progress. Some pupils may need to practise more. If so, incorporate texts from the link reading. This will continually add range and depth.

❦ Ask how well each child is progressing rather than whether you have set enough tasks.

❦ At the 'wings to fly' writing stage, the learning afforded by the taster drafts can be revisited.[3] The focus should be on supporting the retrieval of knowledge.

Tasting is *fun*:

❦ Our schools report so much enjoyment and engagement from taster drafts – they are cognitively challenging yet accessible for every child.

---

3 The phrase 'wings to fly' is used in all the 'Opening Doors' books to refer to the sustained writing stage.

Case study: Taster drafts for impact

Sara Abbas, Mulgrave Primary School, Greenwich, London

At Mulgrave, we use quality texts pitched high for challenge across the school as a means to teach reading and writing. The reason being is that our pupils respond well to the texts we choose, and over time we noticed that their language and vocabulary acquisition was going from strength to strength. What struck me when I began to incorporate the Opening Doors strategies was that it not only enabled us to deepen the children's learning, but it also allowed for deeper engagement early in the writing process, resulting in some great written outcomes.

Upon reading units from the 'Opening Doors' series, I immediately saw the potential of using taster drafts at the beginning stages of the learning journey. Encouraging the children to implement the skills and concepts they had been taught early on allowed the teachers to assess their knowledge and understanding almost immediately. It worked. The prime examples we used were *Pinocchio* and *The Miraculous Journey of Edward Tulane*, which was our core text at the time.

Reading the 'Opening Doors' series back to back for the first time gave me endless possibilities for how to challenge my pupils but also engage them with the writing process, and from then on I saw connections everywhere. The use of taster drafts has enabled me to see how children move from reading to writing using the English taught within and across texts. It has become a clever way to showcase short bursts of writing without holding pupils back and encouraging them to write purely for pleasure, whilst also allowing teachers to gain a deep and meaningful insight into pupils' stages of development as writers.

Short extracts also help teachers to deepen the children's understanding of literary devices, such as extended metaphors, double-echo surprises and pathetic fallacy, which subsequently provides them with rich examples of how to use these in their own writing. Therefore, assessment for learning is immediate and very precise as the feedback given highlights the next steps for each pupil, as well as informs the teacher's future planning based on misconceptions seen or skills that need to be developed further.

Taster drafts also enable pupils at all levels to access and produce writing most suited to their own needs and skillset. Writing freely encourages them to write without constraint, which allows all children to succeed. Some of the most powerful writing has come from some of the most vulnerable and disengaged pupils.

Pupils' work

Sara has been teaching first-person accounts written from the perspective of Bear, linked to the text *The Last Bear* by Hannah Gold. She realised that we don't get to hear the voice of Bear or how he came to lose his family. There are subtle hints to climate change and rising sea levels causing habitat loss and him becoming malnourished, but this is from the voice of April, a little girl who goes to live in the Arctic with her father who is a scientist. Sara began exploring the use of emotive language and language in context. What follows is an example of the process by Aditya Gurung, a Year 2 pupil: an early taster draft exploring the chosen concept and then the second draft.

Early taster draft

I am Bear.

And this, this is my story.

When I was a little cub in the Arctic everything was perfect, we had ice, food supply that was, until the humans took over, they killed my family, and shrunk our cap and we didn't have much food, everything was terrible.

What will happen to me?

Will I be Next?

With No one by my side I had to face the dangers by myself.

I did everything I could to survive …

I scavenged everything I could find, human waste, to rubbish, all of that was barely enough for me.

I depressingly watched my family die out and the humans still going, I was doomed …

Second draft

Devastated, down-cast, alone, I am Bear and my heart is empty.

I've lived in the Arctic Circle for my whole life, ever since I was born, therefore this place is my life.

It is precious to me.

Everything was perfect, because we had an abundance of food supply as well sea ice that was, until humans took over and destroyed our habitat.

Since the beginning of time, we have hunted in packs, however, now we hunt alone, because there are not a lot of us left.

Why do you think this is?

Well, I will tell you what it is that caused my heart to split open, leaving a wide crack deep inside of me, unable to mend or heal no matter what I tried to do.

Now I am all alone with No one to hear me.

My bones are sticking out, protruding from my ribs and my fur is matted with months' dirt.

I am afraid to travel far for long periods of time, because I am too afraid.

All I think about is whether I will live another day, or if I will fade away whilst lonely and afraid.

Who will find me in this empty, vast landscape?

The sky is turning grey as I stand here pondering about the destruction of my home, and whether I will live to see my family again.

Help me. Please.

Resource 14

Chapter 8

Learning Dialogues

Leah Crawford

What ultimately counts [in dialogic teaching] is the extent to which instruction requires students to think, not just to report someone else's thinking.

Martin Nystrand, Adam Gamoran, Robert Kachur and Catherine Prendergast, *Opening Dialogue* (1997)

Language, development and the 'third turn'

Language is the engine in the development of children's intelligence. We learn to think through language. Consider how many young children on entry to school will narrate as they play, narrate their decision-making and will even narrate their reactions as they watch a film or read a book. Those thoughts literally come into being by being externalised in talk.

Teachers who create a truly dialogic classroom recognise that there is no better way to take an X-ray of a child's understanding, and to develop that understanding, than to hear children share their thinking aloud and to respond to their thoughts in ways that can clarify and deepen them. They also recognise that by sharing their ideas aloud, children become more aware of their own thoughts and how they are similar to or different from the thoughts of others.

Of course, the questions you ask and the tasks you set in the classroom are crucial. They enable you to set the high pitch, purposeful agenda that is a central tenet of this book. In order for those quests for meaning to be received as an invitation rather than a demand, it is worth training your class to first turn to a partner or triad to share their emerging ideas with peers.

Let us imagine the moment when you bring the class together and cue in a response (in this case to a sliver of the poem 'Sympathy' by Paul Laurence Dunbar):

Teacher: Pupil A, what did your group think was the mood of the first stanza?

Pupil A: We thought it was calm and peaceful.

Teacher: Excellent! Yes, thank you.

This initiation, response, feedback (IRF) pattern of dialogue dominates classroom discourse in the western world and is a useful pattern for some forms of teaching. But let us pause and think how else this moment could play out, if the purpose of the teacher's feedback is to clarify and extend the pupils' thinking, not overtly evaluate it:

Teacher: Pupil A, what did your group think was the mood of the first stanza?

Pupil A: We thought it was calm and peaceful.

Teacher: Could you tell us what led you to think that?

Pupil A: Erm, so there's gentle words …

Teacher: … like …

Pupil A: Like 'the wind stirs soft' and 'the river flows' … there's things moving but it's gentle movement.

Teacher: Thank you. Can I turn to this group - did you say calm and peaceful or something different?

Pupil B: So, I think this is a bit different. We said it was hopeful and spring-like because it says 'the sun is bright' and you've got the 'first bird sings' and 'first bud' opening, so it's full of life, like life beginning again.

Pupils in this exchange are prompted and supported to clarify, extend and compare – a different, more dynamic and deeper form of feedback than an evaluative 'Yes!' or 'Well done!' which doesn't invite further thinking and might even stymie thought as other pupils listen in and think, 'Well, that wasn't my response – I must be wrong.' The teacher here is trained in the cognitive acceleration programme Let's Think in English, which develops teachers' skills in socially constructing deeper understanding through conceptual challenge and classroom dialogue.[1]

When we explore rich, open and conceptual questions, we need to shift our focus to a fascination with what pupils say and, just as crucially, what you as the teacher will do with what the pupils say – working live and in the moment to make visible and develop their understanding. We will call this the 'power of the third turn' – that is, reframing teacher feedback in IRF exchanges.

Dialogic teaching programmes have had a proven, positive impact on educational outcomes for children – social, emotional and academic. In a webinar for the Chartered College of Teaching in November 2020, Robin Alexander (2020b) was asked to explain the active ingredients of dialogic teaching which have led to this impact. He named three X factors:

1. Pupils are invited and expected to report their thinking. They feel safe, valued, respected and accountable for sharing this thinking. They contribute.

2. Framing your thoughts aloud – for yourself and for others, noticing similarities and differences – improves metacognition. Pupils over time become better at noticing, directing, monitoring and evaluating their thoughts.

3. The power of the teacher's 'third turn' – how you respond to a pupil's answer that both looks backwards to further unravel where that response came from and looks forward to take it further.

---

1   Let's Think in English is one of the cognitive acceleration programmes that have grown out of King's College London. Using a dialogic mode, and planning for development through Piagetian stages, it is a strong model of how to enable equity of access to conceptual challenge. More details can be found at: https://www. letsthinkinenglish.org.

The difficulty with dialogue

Teachers rarely seem to have a problem accepting these three principles, but many experience and admit to difficulties bringing them to life in the busy, messy, social dynamic of the classroom. Not many pupils will enter your class knowing how to contribute and manage their group talk behaviours in ways that are educationally and democratically productive. Talk patterns and routines need to be taught and monitored in the same way that reading or writing behaviours or skills are taught.

The work of Professor Neil Mercer and his colleagues on the Thinking Together project broke new ground in this area by researching and defining the nature of the talk we need for educationally productive group talk and overtly teaching pupils to adopt productive talk behaviours.[2] They coined the term 'exploratory talk': talk in which pupils' reasoning is visible, uncertainty and differences of opinion are invited and explored, evidence and reasons are given, and the group works towards the most plausible, well-reasoned ideas.

A productive way to build a dialogic culture in your classroom with your pupils is to:

❧ Raise awareness of the importance of talk as a tool for thinking.

❧ Create and agree a set of guidelines for exploratory talk.[3]

❧ Support pupils to monitor progress against the guidelines, setting new priorities as they improve.

❧ Model exploratory talk as a teacher: 'I've been wondering …' 'You've really made me think differently there …' 'Are there other possible responses?'

❧ Set tasks and questions that are challenging enough to encourage pupils to turn to each other for support and open enough to invite a range of responses.

---

2   Teaching materials, further reading and guidance on Thinking Together can be found at: https://thinkingtogether.educ.cam.ac.uk.

3   Examples of talk guidelines and tools that can be used to arrive at and monitor them can be found on the Oracy Cambridge website: https://oracycambridge.org.

Many resources are available on the Oracy Cambridge website and are mirrored in their collaborative work with Voice 21.[4]

The English curriculum as a 'living conversation'

This is a book about teaching the humane discipline of English. This is not the same as teaching literacy – the skills that enable you to read and write – although it does, of course, include these. English as the study, interpretation and creation of all manner of texts is a relatively young discipline, certainly compared to science or philosophy. In his books, *Doing English* (2017) and *Literature: Why It Matters* (2019), Professor Robert Eaglestone invites us to think about English as entering a 'living conversation' about life and what it means to be human through texts. It sounds lofty, but it is true.

Every rich picture book, as much as every poem or Shakespeare play, adds to the living conversation of what it means to be human, and every one of our pupils can contribute to this conversation by reading and by writing their own texts. Readers make meaning by entering into dialogue with a text and, even better, into dialogue with other readers of it. The text's meaning does not exist solely on the page; it needs to be brought to life in the mind of the reader. Its meaning is not fixed; the reader's previous life experiences, reading experiences, language, context and culture will influence the meaning they build.

Dialogue voices: windows into a dialogic classroom

To help you imagine what purposeful, creative dialogic teaching looks like, for the rest of this chapter we are going to enter virtually the classroom of Ellen Glynn, teacher of Year 4 at Overton Primary School in Hampshire. Ellen is teaching the unit 'Voices in an Empty Room', a journey through the poem 'Green Candles' by Humbert Wolfe (Unit 5 in *Opening Doors to a Richer English Curriculum for Ages 6 to 9*).

---

4   Voice 21 is a national oracy education charity which grew out of the work of the free school School 21 in Stratford, London. Their mission is to transform the learning and life chances of young people through talk and a high-quality oracy education. See https://voice21.org.

Ellen has layered objectives for this unit. The ambitious, conceptual objective is for the children to understand how character, drama and atmosphere can be created through dialogue and transpose this into their own writing. She also wants to work on the children's reading fluency – lifting text off the page with meaning and knowing the integral link between how a text is read, its language choices and how it is punctuated.

She starts with these words: 'Shut the door.' In groups of three, the children are asked to find at least three different ways to read this text aloud in ways that change its meaning – thinking through who might be saying it, why and in what context. Already the class need one another. One group performs and another is asked to interpret who the speaker might be and why they might be saying it. Have fun with this yourself! It is amazing how the intent, the message behind these words, can change with volume, tone and intonation. Already, there are different plausible interpretations of each performance. The living conversation is already alive in the classroom.

Selecting their favourite scenario, each group is now asked to punctuate the speech accurately and anchor it with a speech verb (e.g. 'she ordered') and an adverb if they wish (e.g. 'he whispered menacingly'). The groups swap and must read each other's lines using the clues/cues on the page.

As each group performs, Ellen doesn't engage in facile praise as feedback but deepens the group's thinking as readers and writers by asking:

- What was it about the sentence that made you raise your voice at the end/speak louder/speak more slowly?

- Were there other possible ways you could have read the line?

- Writers, what do you think about the way your line was performed?

Think of the layers of learning alive in this classroom. The children are reviewing accurate speech punctuation and spelling rules around adding the suffixes 'ed' for past tense and 'ly' for adverbs. But they are also beginning to create a sense of character, atmosphere and situation: interpreting meaning from each other's writing and seeing that meaning builds from a contingent dialogue between author, text and reader.

Ellen can sense that the children are now ripe and ready for a sliver of the poem:

'She shall come in,' answered the open door,
'And not,' said the room, 'go out any more.'

So, we have a beguiling mystery: a talking door and room and an unknown 'she'. The children are asked to discuss in their groups what this mysterious situation might be and why 'she' might not go out any more. Ideas range from the room wanting to trap her or protect her or maybe welcome her back in. These ideas are accepted at this stage but not evaluated by Ellen. She asks the groups if each idea seems possible and they accept at this stage that all are possible.

Ellen now reveals the opening of the poem and asks the children to rethink – which idea now seems most likely?

'There's someone at the door,' said gold candlestick:
'Let her in quick, let her in quick!'
'There is a small hand groping at the handle.'
'Why don't you turn it?' asked green candle.

Here is what plays out in the classroom:

EG: So, let's hear from this group. A – can you share your group's idea?

Pupil A: We think she was captured and now she's escaped.

EG: What made you think that?

Pupil A: Well, like, the room, no, sorry, the candlestick, really wants her to come in because it says 'Let her in quick,' so maybe it's saving her.

EG: Thank you. The rest of the group – is there any other evidence that suggests she's escaped?

Pupil A's group: Erm … [looking at poem … silence]

EG: Maybe we could all look at this. Is there anything else that suggests she's been captured somewhere and is escaping back to the room … [gives time for all pupils to reread] Yes – Pupil B.

Pupil B: Well, she's groping at the handle which could mean she's a bit panicky and wants to get in.

EG: That's helpful, thank you. How about this group – did you have a different idea to A's group?

Pupil C: Yeah, so we think she's gone out without permission and the room wants to get her back in and trap her.

EG: Because … ?

Pupil C: Because … so … the 'Let her in quick' does suggest that they want her back, but then the 'not go out any more' is just a bit spooky. It's a bit weird to never let her go out again.

EG: Interesting – so let's test this out a bit more. How about the groping at the handle that pupil B mentioned? Yes – pupil D, can you pick this up …

Pupil D: So, that might be … so she might be nervous to come back in and her hands are sweaty and slippery.

EG: And she'd be nervous because … ?

Pupil D: … she knows the room is going to be cross with her.

Pupil A: Oh, that actually makes sense!

EG: Thanks. Pupil A – why does that make sense?

The dialogue continues as the class explore more ideas about the 'house' being lonely or controlling. When the whole poem is revealed, the children are ready to attend to more text and more evidence and are able to test out and track their ideas, deciding which one seems most plausible.

How is Ellen supporting deep learning to occur through dialogue? Try to answer this question for yourself based on the insights you have gained from this chapter – into this learning journey and Ellen's live delivery of it here. Think about:

❧ The culture of small group and whole group talk that has been built in this classroom before this learning event.

❧ The nature of Ellen's third turns – what is the nature of her feedback to pupil responses? What impact does it have on learning?

❧ What Ellen's approach is implicitly teaching the pupils about the nature of building meaning as readers and writers.

Visit the Crown House Publishing website to read the incredibly skilful poems written by Ellen Glynn and Dani Morgan's classes: https://www.crownhouse.co.uk/opening-doors-to-a-richer-english-curriculum-pupils-work-ages-6-9-inspired-by-part-1-unit-5.

Link reading

Units that specifically open up dialogue about voices, mood and tone:

❧ The unit used by Ellen and Dani at Overton Primary was 'Voices in an Empty Room' featuring 'Green Candles' by Humbert Wolfe (Unit 5 in *Opening Doors to a Richer English Curriculum for Ages 6 to 9*). This link takes you to a tutorial on Crown House Publishing's YouTube channel: https://www.youtube.com/watch?v=eX5Jg7CjFEU&list=PLxCgNvQM8mbQK9KZ3P5UtQ5dmy5uQrRAX&index=7.

❧ 'The Call' by Charlotte Mew (Unit 1 in *Opening Doors to Famous Poetry and Prose*)

❧ *Great Expectations* by Charles Dickens (Unit 8 in *Opening Doors to Famous Poetry and Prose*)

❧ 'Overheard on a Saltmarsh' by Harold Monro (Unit 5 in *Opening Doors to Quality Writing for Ages 6 to 9*)

❧ 'Lonely Street' by Francisco López Merino (Unit 8 in *Opening Doors to Quality Writing for Ages 6 to 9*)

❧ 'Hurt No Living Thing' by Christina Rossetti (Unit 3 in *Opening Doors to a Richer English Curriculum for Ages 6 to 9*)

❧ *Pinocchio* by Carlo Collodi (Unit 13 in *Opening Doors to a Richer English Curriculum for Ages 6 to 9*)

❧ 'The Door' by Miroslav Holub (Unit 1 in *Opening Doors to a Richer English Curriculum for Ages 10 to 13*)

❧ 'Sympathy' by Paul Laurence Dunbar (Unit 5 in *Opening Doors to a Richer English Curriculum for Ages 10 to 13*)

Key points on using learning dialogues

Build a *safe and collaborative culture* of high participation and respectful listening.

Plan *rich questions and tasks* that provide engaging challenge and open the need for dialogic enquiry.

Scaffold *extended contributions* that clarify, reason and provide evidence through the third turn.

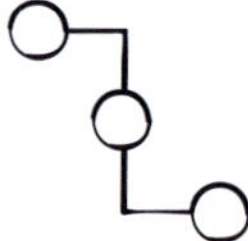

Steer classroom dialogue into *chains of enquiry* – encouraging pupils to respond to each other's ideas, building and challenging.

Build knowledge in English through pupils' *conversations with the text*, with each other and with other readers through time.

Case study: Building a dialogic learning community through the year

Ellen Glynn, Overton Church of England Primary School, Overton, Hampshire

Developing a space where children engage in rich dialogic talk means carefully considering who works together. We have 'reading trios' – three mixed-ability children talking and sharing ideas. While the children are talking together, I will circle round and listen in on their conversations. I try not to make eye contact during this time as the children then start talking to me rather than to their group. But, at the start of the year, I always tell them that I am only eavesdropping and they must pretend that I am not there. They soon learn to ignore me! I listen in so the children know that I am interested in their discussion, and so I can gauge their understanding and make decisions about which group I want to share first. This isn't the group with the strongest answer. I choose the group that might just be grasping understanding: enough there but still needs work – a rich starting point.

The expectation is that every child knows they might be called on to give a response for their group, so we agree no hands up and I generally ask the less vocal children first. This means their ideas won't yet have been heard and they will have had time to formulate a response with their group, so the pressure is off them to think of something to say. Then I mop up with the more confident children, asking for ideas that have not been mentioned. This approach stretches them and ensures they dig deeper for the not-so-obvious responses, and it allows all the children to see that the more confident among them are not the ones with all the answers. For children who really struggle to speak out, I quietly tell them that I am going to come to them first and to indicate to me when they are ready to speak.

I teach the children some sentence starters using the pronoun 'we' such as: 'We thought …' 'We agree with … because …' 'We respectfully disagree with … because …' This gives the less confident children a way in, and also takes the fear out of giving an answer because the response is collective and not personal. I don't give my own opinion during these sessions; rather, I take on the position of a curious listener and encourager to talk more, modelling the behaviours I want to see from them. I will encourage the children to respond to each other directly, rather than to me, by using phrases like 'Tell us what your group was thinking' and teaching them to look at their peers rather than at me.

I am happy with silence – silence waiting to be filled with a response. I don't rush in to scaffold or prompt unless it is really necessary, and this would be a clarifying question rather than a new one. I don't make judgements about their answers but respond with phrases like, 'Tell us more …' 'What made your group think that?' 'Would anyone like to add to this?' 'Are there any groups who have a different idea?' 'Tell us how you arrived at that …'

I will support the class to keep track of all the ideas by doing a quick summary every now and again: 'So, this is what we're thinking at the moment …' The use of collective pronouns is important as it shows the children that we are building understanding together rather than a few children having the 'right answer'. It is important for groups to justify their responses with evidence from the text. However, if their responses are a bit 'off' then rather than tell them it isn't right, I might ask, 'What was it in the text that made you think that?' or 'At what point in the text did you come to that decision?' This forces them to look more closely at the text and re-evaluate their own answer rather than relying on me to do so.

The aim of the session is always to make meaning together rather than arrive at a predetermined answer. When children are encouraged and supported to explore and evaluate their own thinking, without overt judgement, they become more confident in expressing their ideas and are more willing to change them in light of the evidence.

Chapter 9

Excellence Success Criteria

Bob Cox

Of course, writing tools need to be taught, but the starting point should be the key success pointers of any good writing: the author's intent and the impact on the reader. …

Success criteria in writing do not guarantee quality, only inclusion. Quality comes from children's own reading experiences being applied and the all-important class analysis of what good writing looks like.

Shirley Clarke, *Formative Assessment: A Little Guide for Teachers* (2021)

How can pitch-high mindsets be applied to assessment and tap into the dynamic potential it has to influence the next steps of the curriculum? Too often, pupils look back at the assessment criteria or national curriculum tick lists and manipulate aspects of grammar or punctuation to fulfil their teachers' expectations. The flow and creativity of the writing can be lost.[1] If this becomes a policy, an assessment-driven curriculum can result. Teachers (and pupils) end up constantly ensuring the artificial coverage of criteria rather than teaching new knowledge.

Government benchmarking of schools via league tables, a discrete spelling, punctuation and grammar test and SATs has not helped. I have seen schools that are attempting to fulfil the latest assessment criteria descend into a tailspin, like journeying on a switchback road: some progress is made but there is a loss of forward momentum.

However, many schools are showing that assessment can be utilised in ways that spur on new learning by diagnosing gaps and supporting teachers to find the best way forward for each child. They are still

---

1 Brain flow is the state of mind that occurs when a person is fully absorbed in an activity. For more on flow, see the work of Mihaly Csikszentmihalyi listed at: https://www.cgu.edu/people/mihaly-csikszentmihalyi.

Resource 15

achieving high SATs results, including greater depth scores. Assessment is there to inspire fresh planning and momentum, not to control the lesson plan. Just as we should plan to challenge the most able pupils first – planning to and beyond the top – so we can start our assessment thinking with the maximum ambition.

Always try to plan the hardest criteria that can be assessed first, which will enable you to gauge the scope of the text you are using. Planning content and assessment from the top can benefit the aspirations behind your curriculum thinking. You can then layer in interventions and support as appropriate, with maximum scaffolding according to need, not prior labelling.

The curriculum can be a key driver to progression, with assessment revealing the potential for next steps or the exact areas where revisiting and further practice may be needed.

How can excellence criteria be applied?

To discover how assessment can be more ambitious and have more impact on learning, take a look at this extract from the superb *Where the River Runs Gold* by Sita Brahmachari. Shifa is on the run from a life in an imaginary near future where most children are used for pollination labour in the absence of bees and the only privileges are left for the few. You might consider starting by using the illustration with a topic sentence starter: 'Once inside, all three of them leaned against the boulder, too exhausted to move a step further.'

❦ What puzzles you about the picture?

❦ What kind of description will this be?

❦ What will the mood or tone of the writing be?

If your pupils write a taster draft based on a scene in a tunnel, they can compare it with the passage below written in Sita Brahmachari's superb prose.

Shifa, Themba and Luca are climbing through a gap between a boulder and a tunnel roof:

Once inside, all three of them leaned against the boulder, too exhausted to move a step further. Shifa crouched low and felt for what was under her feet. It seemed like they were standing on some kind of lever that now creaked under their weight. Shifa felt the urge to jump off. Too late as the boulder shifted and a deep rumble swelled around them; the gale built to its crescendo. A lightning flash and a huge crash shattered the tunnel, bricks and boulders flew in all directions. They crouched, protecting their heads. Shifa felt the earth groan and crack under their feet. The second wave of the storm transformed the loosened boulder into a plug that now shunted them further into the tunnel. Shifa squinted up just in time to catch the narrowing crack of sky between the flower tracks and the tunnel roof close as the last bats shot in, their animal and human cries as one. They clasped each other's hands as they were propelled into the deepening darkness. The tunnel echoed with the screech of winged and human fear. (p. 294)

This passage could be part of a multilayered aim to teach how a narrative can explode into action, with setting and character complementing one another. The concept could be building narrative power, and the deep objectives could be:

❦ Reading: How does the author build action and adventure through narrative power in this passage?

❦ Writing: How well can you create the same kind of narrative power in your own story?

The rich objectives will emphasise the scope in a challenging text for depth and interactions with new knowledge. The same big questions could be asked at degree level, but with vastly more complex texts. Thus, the primary phase can become a playground for innovation without boundaries, at the same time as embedding the basics in the most fascinating of contexts.

The radial layout (see Chapter 10) might look like this:

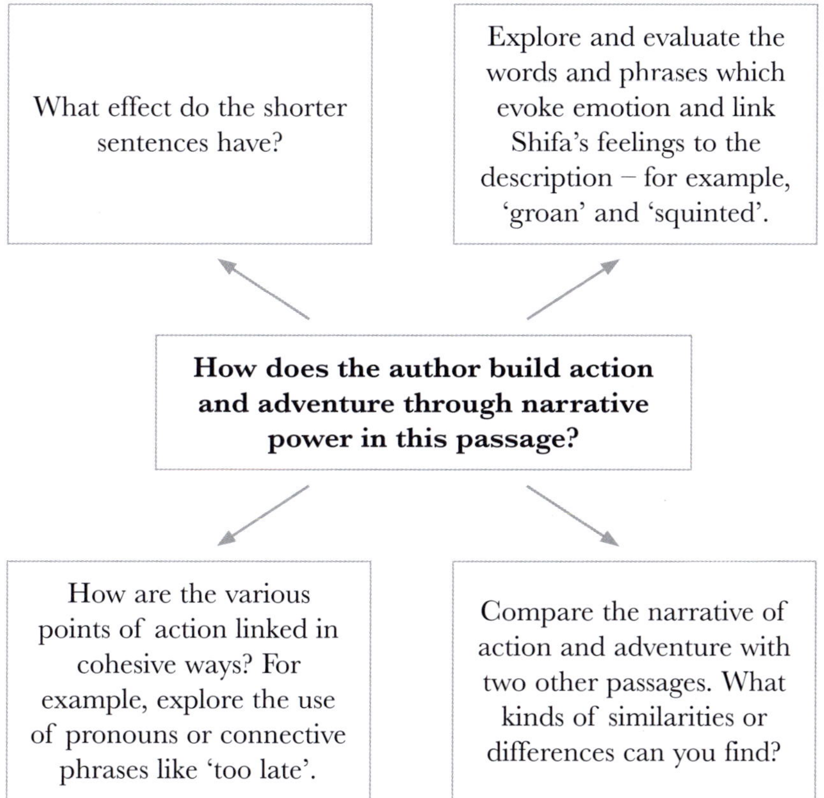

The four boxes in this example correspond to important aspects of English: structure, cohesion, figurative language and intertextuality. These can be broken down in turn, if you wish, into teaching aims, which might include adverbials, noun phrases, metaphor and so on.

Increasingly, spelling is being taught in context. The double 'l' in 'swelled' or the 'sc' in 'crescendo' would be two examples where you could combine a focus on spelling with the meaning of the word as it contributes to the action. Contextualisation is more likely to lodge learning in the long-term memory.

When you are teaching about the concept of narrative power, you might use the following elements to influence your teaching and assessment. I have deliberately used question cues rather than answers to guide your thinking.

Excellent responses will:

Explore how structure supports meaning:

❦ How do the shorter sentences add focus like a zoom lens on a camera?

❦ Can you show how Shifa's feelings link with changing action?

❦ How does the rising description of the perils in the cave reflect the increasing threat?

❦ Why are the bats important?

Show how cohesion adds to the rising tension:

❦ Why are Shifa's emotions important?

❦ What kinds of effective linking can you explore, like the use of pronouns or phrases connecting with the previous sentence?

❦ How do the connections add to the rising crescendo of the gale through the passage?

Explain how well figurative language is used:

❦ How do figures of speech enhance the narrative power?

❦ Alliteration?

❦ Metaphor?

Include examples of contrasting powerful narratives from other texts:

❦ Explain how other passages displaying narrative power are both similar and different.

❦ How has structure, cohesion and figurative language played its part in each example?

We have always emphasised that excellence success criteria should be for the understanding of the teacher first. Work through the aspects of structure, cohesion and language study in your own mind, using the statements above to help you, and only then articulate assessment demands for your pupils, at the right time and woven into your teaching. The criteria and their associated expectations only take on meaning via learning dialogues and questioning, but your awareness of the knowledge potential in a passage is critical. It will drive your questions, your momentum and your confidence. Each time you use the text your confidence will grow, so don't expect a mastery of the text first time round.

Above all, the aspects of English used in this example should not be presented as a tick list. The wonderful flow of the prose can be preserved whilst still deepening understanding of specific aspects of English. It is more about appreciating the language and fluency of reading as the words hit the imagination; sophisticated technique can support ease of communication rather than becoming words to highlight and move on.

Stages on the road to excellence

With more knowledge comes less need for planning, and supplementary questions can be set according to the answers the pupils give. As the epigraph from Shirley Clarke at the start of the chapter observes, it is the skill and knowledge of the teacher that turns criteria statements or lists into something that lives creatively in the classroom. Find your own child-friendly talk that suits your pupils when you articulate the potential for excellent responses, but the thinking you have done to produce the list will have taken your ambitions for them a bit deeper.

Consequently, when it comes to assessment, you can start not just your planning but also your thinking right at the top. The hardest assessment bullet point doesn't have to come last. You will see the phrase 'Excellent responses will …' in constant use across the units in both volumes of the *Opening Doors to a Richer English Curriculum* books.

The concept comes first, followed by the open-ended excellence criteria and then your own focus on functional aspects of English. Under structure in *Where the River Runs Gold*, to give just one example, you might want to teach more about:

❦ Summary skills in three sections: the initial description, the second wave, and then bats and humans linked.

❦ Use of verbs – for example, 'squinted' to give the limited view that we too get as a reader.

If you understand and articulate the potential for excellence in comprehension work or creative writing, then assessment expectations become aspirational rather than itemised, reflected on rather than copied down, and discussed rather than posted on the board. Gradually, all your pupils will acquire enough knowledge to start building full and well-argued answers to the question of narrative power, and there will certainly be a place for apportioning marks and then there will certainly be benchmarking progress against the criteria.

The four radial boxes will help you to ensure that you teach the relevant aspects of structure or cohesion in the passage and evaluate how well your pupils are doing on each one. The fine detail on your assessment of their responses will inspire the next steps of learning by revealing gaps in knowledge or understanding.

Link reading

We are constantly looking for opportunities to make links from past to present. Sita Brahmachari's *Where the River Runs Gold* is a science fiction book and an adventure story as well as a modern environmental tale. Intertextual connections could be developed via reference to some of the following texts, with extracts chosen to explore the concept of narrative power:

- *The Wolves of Willoughby Chase* by Joan Aiken (the beginning!)
- *Asha and the Spirit Bird* by Jasbinder Bilan
- *The Longest Night of Charlie Noon* by Christopher Edge
- *The House* by J. Patrick Lewis, illustrated by Roberto Innocenti
- *Children of the Stone City* by Beverley Naidoo
- *Tyger* by S. F. Said, illustrated by Dave Mckean

And from the 'Opening Doors' books:

- *Journey to the Centre of the Earth* by Jules Verne (Unit 10 in *Opening Doors to Famous Poetry and Prose*)
- *The Wizard of Oz* by L. Frank Baum (Unit 14 in *Opening Doors to Quality Writing for Ages 6 to 9*)
- *The Hound of the Baskervilles* by Sir Arthur Conan Doyle (Unit 6 in *Opening Doors to Quality Writing for Ages 10 to 13*)
- 'Over the Hills and Far Away' by Hilary McKay and 'Blackberry Blue' by Jamila Gavin (Unit 8 in *Opening Doors to a Richer English Curriculum for Ages 6 to 9*)

❧ *Little Women* by Louisa May Alcott (Unit 14 in *Opening Doors to a Richer English Curriculum for Ages 10 to 13*)

Key points on excellence success criteria

Plan high pitch *excellence criteria* which will demonstrate a deep understanding of the objectives. Planning from the top means devising the most ambitious criteria first.

Relate the statements to your *concept* or the aspect of English you are teaching.

Map in specific aspects of *functional English* from the national curriculum. They are vital skills and contribute to the impact of the writing overall, but they don't have life or meaning without a context.

Use radial layouts to itemise the *stages* of the journey to excellence. You can then expect your pupils to be more articulate about the big question as they progress. This eventually translates into improved written answers.

Use *assessment data* to inspire excellence for all by pinpointing the next stages in mastering a concept.

Use a range of *learning dialogues* to make sure the journey to excellence is well understood and articulated.

Case study: Excellence success criteria

Wenda Davies, Coastlands County Primary School, St Ishmael's, Pembrokeshire

October 2019. Luke – a sometimes reluctant Year 5 writer – is self-assessing his personification poem against the listed success criteria. The children had been working up to this piece for several lessons – reading a range of poems that personify the wind, including Dionne Brand's 'Wind' (Unit 1 in *Opening Doors to a Richer English Curriculum for Ages 6 to 9*) and Ted Hughes' rich and challenging poem also entitled 'Wind'. We had drawn up the success criteria together, following class discussion of the texts:

- I can give my chosen subject a distinct personality – e.g. playful, lonely, angry.

- I can choose verbs carefully to describe what my subject does.

- I can make my subject/character change as the poem progresses.

- Challenge: I can write in the form of a sonnet.

I circulate the class as they review their work. Most of the children have chosen to personify an elemental aspect of the natural world like the sea or fire. Luke has made a more unusual choice – his poem is about colours, including lines like, 'I am the tip of the waves, / Creamy-white and frothy'. Filling out his self-assessment slip, Luke is clearly aware that his poem doesn't follow the success criteria. As I walk by, he looks up, shrugs his shoulders and says to me, 'But it's still a good poem.' And yes – it was!

By this point, we had been using the 'Opening Doors' books for some years. The children were really thriving on a diet of rich, challenging texts and the culture of high expectations for everyone that the Opening Doors approach embraces. But it was clear that our approach of tick-list-style success criteria needed rethinking. Luke could have gone back to his work and shoe-horned in some extra verbs or tinkered with the number of lines, so he had fourteen of them, but would this have led to a better poem?

We looked again to the Opening Doors materials, noticing how the units suggest what would be 'excellent responses' to the rich texts on offer. Combining this with the radial layout also featured in the books, we began to adapt our approach towards success criteria. Instead of it being a list to work through and tick off, we started to tease out from the stimulus text what made it effective and set these as aspirations for our own writing, under the guise of 'Excellent responses might include …'

In recent work on the ending of *Alice's Adventures in Wonderland* – when Alice's sister goes into a dream-like reverie – we unpicked how Lewis Carroll had effectively linked the real and dream worlds, and the children worked from the following excellence success criteria:

Excellent responses might include:

The use of extended sentences, punctuated by dashes.	**How well can I create my own dream world and link it with the real world in my narrative?**	The use of the conditional tense – *would change, would be.*
The action is seen through the character's eyes – *she just knew …*	Appealing to the senses – hearing, touch.	The pairing of nouns in the real and dream world.

This led to the following imaginative taster draft by Harry, in Year 4:

So he sat with closed eyes, and half-believed himself in the Forbidden Forest, though he knew that if he were only to open them again he would be back by the dank pool in his garden with its weed swaying sadly in the water – the water dragon would change to the dull brown pike, and the mad moose's howl would be the deer's slow hooves shuffling – and the place of the phoenix flying through the trees would be taken by the jumping frogs, while the delicate silk of the spider webs would change (he just knew) to the soft mud at the pond's edge.

But what impact is this approach having on standards? In our present Year 6 cohort, 87.5% of learners reached Level 5+ in writing. This compares to our pre-pandemic results of 75% at Level 5+. There is no doubt that, through our use of co-constructed excellence success criteria, our learners are crafting more effective, original and authentic work. Rather than a tick list linked to levels or age-related expectations, they are focusing more on the impact of their writing on the reader. And they are all aiming high!

Chapter 10

Radial Question Layouts

Bob Cox

Comprehension strategies should be taught – and, according to research, should be taught using a gradual release of responsibility approach. That just means that the teacher models and explains when, how, and why to implement the strategies.

Timothy Shanahan, 'Where Questioning Fits in Comprehension Instruction' (2018)

Teaching is such a demanding job that it is unsurprising that certain routines, which offer familiarity and speed of planning, have become popular in primary classrooms over the years. Examples in English might be comprehension books offering various passages along with lists of questions to answer or cloze-type exercises that require set answers to grammatical conundrums.

To dip into such activities may be practical and pragmatic, even occasionally useful, but if it becomes a set habit of delivery, then we need to question whether this is ambitious enough for a rich English curriculum. Furthermore, is wading through comprehension skills books or worksheets offering genuine opportunities for talking, exploring or teaching? The Shanahan approach, outlined above, proposes using specific strategies to teach new knowledge. As pupils' autonomy grows, so too does their confidence to read and interrogate other challenging texts.

In fact, there is growing evidence that it is hard to transfer comprehension skills to fresh contexts, and therefore any attempt to train pupils to spot types of questions is in vain. Shanahan (2018) argues for there to be differentiation between skills and strategies: 'Skills practice is a time waster. It's like pushing the elevator button twice.' He then advises on what kinds of approaches might work – for

Resource 17

example, engaging pupils in discussions about the texts themselves, and not about lists of skills.

This neatly summarises the kinds of relationships with texts we have worked on with our schools. Specific instruction and learning dialogues should be part of a teacher's repertoire for activating comprehension journeys. This may include a focus on:

- Fluency and meaning.
- Linking connotations to form patterns.
- Understanding multiple contexts for vocabulary usage.
- Exploring the many ways in which meaning is inferred.
- Continuously linking in whole-text reading, often on the same concept or theme.
- Deepening appreciation, wonder and reading for pleasure.

To summarise, you are seeking to encourage your pupils to enter into a relationship with a text. The interest sparked by your discussions, dialogues and debates will be inspiring and enriching – and it is ambitious texts that will provide the most opportunities for such discourse to open doors to new knowledge.

Follow a popular instructional theory by all means, but don't allow the steps to control or limit you. The potential of your challenging text, pitched just above the standard of your most advanced pupil, is the beginning of your pupils' route to excellence. Your own mastery of that text signals more autonomy and more freedom to be creative.

Changing classroom practice

What kind of structure can be developed, particularly with questioning and additional thinking prompts in mind?

In my consultancy role, observing language study in action across hundreds of classrooms, I noticed limitations with the linear nature of questions set for children about their reading. Time and again, there was a lack of flexibility in matching question to pupil.

The linear sequencing of questions raised a number of issues:

- The habit of setting questions moving from easy to hard did not promote thinking from teacher or pupil. It was an exercise to complete or a test. This strategy might make sense in a formal situation when reassurance and confidence-building is needed at the start (we see this on *Mastermind*, for example), but why is this necessary in teaching situations involving new knowledge acquisition and dialogic approaches?

- The skills practice was not transferable to other texts. If the idea was to spot and identify question types, then it was in vain because it is engaging with meaning via the text itself that is valuable. And each text is different.

- The preliminary questions were too easy for advanced pupils.

- By the time advanced pupils reached the later questions, requiring deeper thinking and more challenging connections, time was running out.

- Pupils with lower reading ages were not experiencing open, complex questions because they rarely got beyond the middle challenges. This is a kind of deprivation, as they are then likely to be fazed by such questions when they encounter them in a test or formal situation. Teachers may also make the judgement that they cannot answer challenging questions fully when, in fact, they may never have had the chance to attempt them.

- There was a lack of a learning dialogue between teacher and pupils. There was a more formal demand for answers rather than opportunities to revel in the challenge of a question or learn and explore language.

Gradually, I was able to trial with schools a way of enabling all pupils to interact with more questions and to work in stages towards a very ambitious big question. The strategy has come to be called 'radial layouts': linear ladders have been replaced with a big Opening Doors question in the centre and a range of supplementary challenges around the outside. Some schools have called the big question a 'javelin question' to signify a challenge thrown high into the air!

Let us take an example to illustrate what I mean and how this can influence your planning.

In Michael Morpurgo's *I Believe in Unicorns*, 8-year-old Tomas Porec, growing up in a mountain village, begins to take an interest in reading for the first time by listening to the so-called 'Unicorn Lady' who reads stories in the library with a large wooden unicorn sitting beside her. One day, Tomas takes his turn to read whilst sitting on the unicorn:

'*The Little Match Girl* also happens to be a lovely story, children; very sad but very lovely. Tomas, I wonder if you'd like to come and sit on the unicorn and read it to us. You haven't had a turn on the unicorn yet, have you?' Everyone was looking at me.

They were waiting. My mouth was dry. I couldn't do it. I was filled with sudden fear.

'Come on,' she said. 'Come and sit beside me on the unicorn.'

I had never been any good at reading out loud at school. I would forever stutter over my consonants – I dreaded *k*'s in particular. Long words terrified me in case I pronounced them wrongly and everyone laughed at me. But now, sitting up there on the magic unicorn, I began to read, and all my dread and all my terror simply vanished. I heard my voice speaking out strong and loud. It was as if I was up in the mountains alone and singing a song at the top of my voice, for the sheer joy of the sound of it. The words danced like music on the air, and I could feel everyone listening. And I knew they were listening not to me at all, but to the story of *The Little Match Girl*, because they were just as lost in it as I was.

That same day I borrowed my first book from the library.

(p. 53)

Instead of using this passage simply to set comprehension questions to benchmark progress, a radial layout of challenges can give you more flexibility and the potential for ambitious thinking. Instead of practising skills centred around types of questions – for example, summarising, nuances in vocabulary, explaining or retrieving knowledge – this strategy hinges around ways of responding to a text to glean more knowledge and more meaning.

Take the following example:

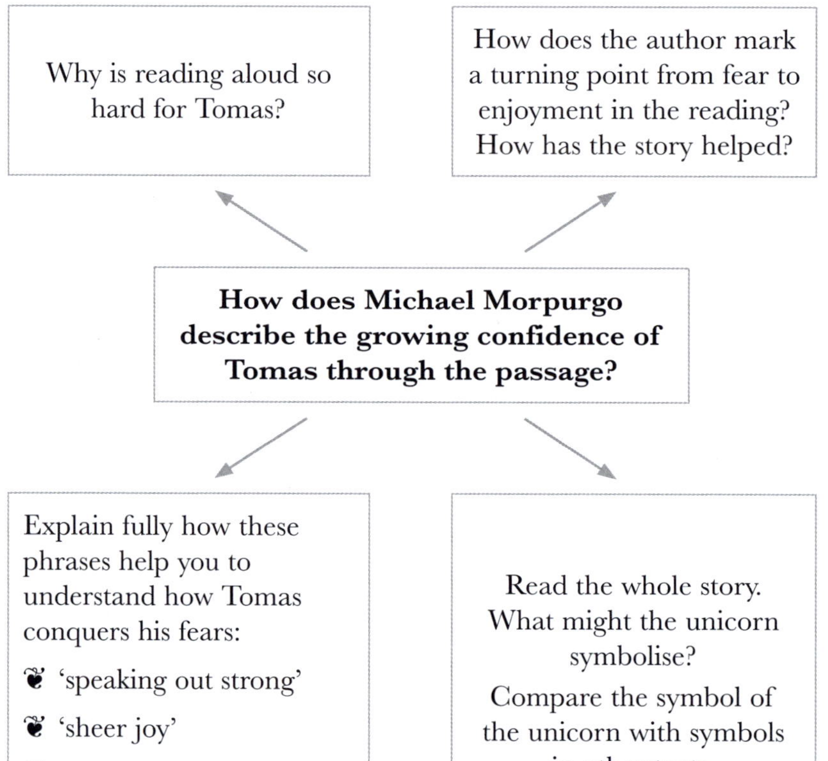

When devising a conventional list of linear questions, running from relatively easy to relatively hard, a central big question is often not set. If it can be found at all, it is always at the end of the sequence and even advanced pupils may not start on the question before the time has run out.

As long as there has been in-depth teaching, with new knowledge explained and explored in chunks prior to the radial layouts being presented, our schools are finding that the big Opening Doors question can be set up front.

Graham Nuthall's seminal work, *The Hidden Lives of Learners* (2007: 162), which utilises a lifetime of research, closes with a section on 'What is learning?', which includes this finding on big questions:

'Because learning takes time, it is better to invest teaching time and resources in a smaller number of big questions or problems in depth, rather than covering every aspect of the curriculum at a surface level of understanding.'

The supplementary questions feed the big question, providing access and enjoyment – a reading journey to explore a concept rather than yet another exercise. Radial questions are not designed to be set as tests. They are a tool for further teaching and interventions by you and teaching assistants, with easier questions set if more scaffolding is needed. For example, when explaining the four phrases relating to Tomas' fears, you may wish to find out how much the pupils understand initially before exploring a word like 'lost' and its many different connotations.

The advantages of radial layouts include:

❦ By chunking stages of understanding, they enable you to focus on the different aspects of new knowledge and learning that arise in the passage. Understanding grows via the question responses and direct teaching, building up the pupils' ability to construct a detailed answer for the big Opening Doors question.

❦ They can help you to group pupils according to need and guide their development; the groupings can alter according to the progress made. It is a flexible way to utilise the advantages of guided reading without the labelling. Teaching via challenges often prompts new thinking in our schools about 'ability'. Pupils are moved on when they have demonstrated an understanding of the vocabulary explanations, for example, not because of a prior reading score. There are no presuppositions.

❦ The challenge is endemic but the language is accessible via your tuition.

❦ All pupils can share the same objective *and* access the power of the narrative.

❦ Easier questions can be added if the pupils are stuck. This should happen if necessary, but it should not be programmed in as an expectation.

❦ You can produce the supplementary support questions as coloured cards and hand them out according to need.

❦ Pupils who find literacy hard never feel they are being given easy questions – just the same questions as others, whilst more advanced pupils are routinely immersed in challenging language. As we emphasise throughout the 'Opening Doors' series, a diverse range of access strategies can function like keys to unlock the unpredictability of the mind and open up opportunity for all: equity and excellence.

❦ Connections with link reading selections (see Chapter 6) can be made throughout the process.

Comprehension can be turned into a real joy – a journey of learning and discovery, not a drab routine of exercises. And it is the talent of teachers that brings the reading alive for pupils.

At first, it may be beneficial to ask your pupils to identify links and connections within a single text before encouraging them to make contrasts and comparisons across the link reading. Learning how to find themes, explore new vocabulary and boldly confront unknown terminology or word usage in one text is more likely to build their confidence and facilitate the transference of that understanding to a new topic or text.

Natalie Wexler, the co-author with Judith Hochman of *The Writing Revolution* (2017), states:

> At lower grade levels children read texts that don't use much sophisticated vocabulary, and students may figure out what kinds of answers teachers are looking for … Years later, when texts assume academic knowledge and vocabulary that kids haven't been taught, they often struggle. (Wexler, 2022a)

The more we use quality texts and associated language study within an ethos of exploration and questioning, the more chance there is that pupils will be ready to interact with complex aspects of English later on.

The big picture: inclusion and excellence

Every single pupil can be part of the journey because every single pupil is experiencing challenge. Where there is a need for support it can be given, but expectations are always high. Radial question layouts around a big conceptual conundrum should move knowledge onwards via scaffolding, teacher prompts and breakthrough opportunities.

Here are some examples showing how support questions – challenging in themselves – can deepen pupils' learning and build knowledge acquisition for the comprehension needed to attempt a big Opening Doors question:

- **Fluency** – the wonderful extract from *I Believe in Unicorns* is perfect for reading aloud – and what a great opportunity for the pupils to echo read sections![1] I would recommend HFL Education's superb and innovative work on fluency and commend the differences their staff and teachers are making.[2]

- **Vocabulary development** – for example, by linking Tomas' dry mouth with 'dread' and 'terror'. You may enjoy Kelly Ashley's book *Word Power* (2019) which explores numerous ways of teaching children about words.

- **Spelling development** – by considering the frequent 'ea' combination in 'read' and 'dread' and the double 'r' in 'terror'. There is huge scope for more spelling, grammar and punctuation work in context.

- **Concepts** – exploring the use of a first-person narrator could be the driver for many other aspects of English in this passage, such as: emotional engagement, a reader's viewpoint via a narrator and sentence connections as links with the narrator's feelings.

As the cognitive field of learning builds like a matrix, you can assess which pupils are ready for the greater depth challenge, which in the Morpurgo example requires knowledge of the use of symbols in other texts. The link reading will be relevant to answering the central

---

1 Echo reading is when pupils repeat phrases or sentences after a teacher has read them, providing opportunities for tuition and fluency improvement.

2 See https://www.hertsforlearning.co.uk/teaching-and-learning/research-projects/english-research-projects.

open question too, as all the connections made about symbols via intertextuality will encourage in-depth answers. Most pupils should reach the question with the highest demands at some point – and remember that *all* oral and written responses to the support questions contribute to the big question. In line with Shanahan's research, encourage maximum independence by finding out which pupils can attempt the big question without the help of (at least some of) the supplementary questions.

Opening Doors is a flexible system. Rigid approaches tend to presume that all schools can deliver or roll out the same learning in the same way. I have worked with schools in the same area over a long period of time, and even then each school is very different. Applying and adapting big principles gives teachers the chance to develop shared rationales for English, but also leave space for adaptation and creativity – a structure with gaps. By planning with big principles in mind and using a strategy like radial layouts as a tool, you can intervene in personalised ways according to need, inventing new questions if it is necessary.

Pitch high and scaffold accordingly rather than starting with the obvious and finding that ambitious questions are rarely attempted. Of course, it is the scope and beauty of the writing that is such a gift for the teacher of English!

Link reading

Examples of radial layouts can be found throughout the 'Opening Doors' series, but the following units include examples that our schools have found particularly useful:

- ❦ 'Prince Kano' by Edward Lowbury (Unit 6 in *Opening Doors to a Richer English Curriculum for Ages 6 to 9*)

- ❦ *The American Woman's Home* by Catherine E. Beecher and Harriet Beecher Stowe (Unit 11 in *Opening Doors to a Richer English Curriculum for Ages 6 to 9*)

- ❦ *The Story of the Blue Planet* by Andri Snær Magnason (Unit 15 in *Opening Doors to a Richer English Curriculum for Ages 6 to 9*)

- ❦ 'Speak of the North!' by Charlotte Brontë (Unit 2 in *Opening Doors to a Richer English Curriculum for Ages 10 to 13*)

- ❦ 'Sympathy' by Paul Laurence Dunbar (Unit 5 in *Opening Doors to a Richer English Curriculum for Ages 10 to 13*)

- ❦ Fake News – In Search of the Truth (Unit 15 in *Opening Doors to a Richer English Curriculum for Ages 10 to 13*)

Key points on using radial layouts

Use a *challenging text* with scope for learning or the questions won't probe deep enough.

Devise the big Opening Doors question first with plenty of scope to explore a 'how' or 'why' conundrum. This is planning from the top.

Find more opportunities for *direct tuition* and knowledge-building via the support questions.

Exploit more opportunities for *learning dialogues,* oracy and interventions as groups or individuals explore the support questions.

Routes towards the detailed answering of an *ambitious open question* can be stepped and evaluated. Each chunk of knowledge can relate to the next one and responses to the big question will build.

Appropriate routes can be found for each individual *through the level of progress they actually make* rather than pre-planned labelling. This applies to advanced learners too.

Radial layouts can be a tool to facilitate *equity and excellence.*

Case study: Using radial layouts for equity and excellence

Jacob Wahab, Ravensworth Primary School, Mottingham, London

At Ravensworth Primary School, we have used radial layouts as part of our English teaching sequences for some time and have found that they work really well.

When we talk about English as practitioners, we often forget that it is made up of three strands – reading, writing and oracy. It is the oracy aspect that can be overlooked in the relentless drive for progress. Whilst some schools are choosing to reduce the amount of drama and deep discussion going on in the classroom, we believe that we should be doing the opposite and pushing for more.

Radial questions provide children with opportunities to grapple with deep thinking and require advanced comprehension skills. Not only this, but we have found that our more disadvantaged pupils (or the horribly named 'less able') are able to access higher order thinking questions that were previously believed to be beyond them. The radial approach is successful because it breaks the question down into smaller chunks that the children can unpick and collect evidence for before drawing their conclusions.

For example, when you place a daunting text like Edgar Allan Poe's narrative poem 'The Raven'[3] in front of a room of 10-year-olds, many would predict that even greater depth children would struggle. But when you have a laser focus on a singular aspect and slowly expand it to the larger picture, the children can suddenly grasp content that is beyond their reading age. You then spot certain phrases reappearing in their writing, carefully considered repetition and conscious control of their vocabulary to create the desired atmosphere.

---

3   See https://www.poetryfoundation.org/poems/48860/the-raven.

This is a variation on the opening of 'The Raven':

Once upon a midnight dreary,

I wandered weak and weary,

Whilst I ponder about the yonder of faraway …

I nod, a nearly napping

When there came a tapping,

A

Tap

Tap

Tapping at my chamber door.

It was then

Whilst staring into the fiery ember of December,

Oh, how I remember

A beautiful dove landed on my floor.

Adam (Year 6)

When combined with the link reading, radial questions produce so much more depth and the children begin to think creatively. This is when the exciting connections happen and the children make links that we could not have anticipated.

Since using these strategies, the number of our pupils achieving age-related expectations has increased, but it is actually our greater depth percentages that have shot up the most. On average, around 20% of the cohort achieve greater depth every year, and we believe that radial questions play a large part in this.

Part 3
Further Applications

Resource 19

Chapter 11

Opening Doors at Key Stage 1

Julie Sargent

To truly ensure our students' success, we must expose them to complex (or a least pre-complex) texts relatively early and relatively often, including during their elementary and middle school years, while there is time to steadily and gradually develop their comfort and skill with the various types of challenge these texts create.

Doug Lemov, Colleen Driggs and Erica Woolway,
***Reading Reconsidered* (2016)**

What does our curriculum offer for English look like for our youngest pupils? The current focus on early reading emphasises the importance of getting provision right from the start. So, how can we ensure that we are providing our Key Stage 1 pupils with sufficient challenge to promote, deepen and develop English? What could the foundations for Key Stage 2 look like? How do we ensure every child can access this?

A key consideration is: why use challenging texts when children are still learning to decode and encode? There is no doubt that it is vital for children to learn to decode and encode to support fluency in reading and writing.[1] As part of this provision, children read decodable texts,[2] which serve a clear purpose in the teaching of reading.

Yet, in these early stages of reading and writing, we need to consider how else to develop the wider elements of English. By exposing all children to a wide range of challenging material, we support them in

---

1 Decode means to identify and blend phonemes to read written words. Encode means to identify phonemes in spoken words and then write the corresponding grapheme (letter or letters).

2 'The term "decodable books" is often used to describe books that have been structured in cumulative steps for children learning to read so that, as their knowledge of the alphabetic code increases, they can decode every word' (Department for Education, 2021: 105).

acquiring new vocabulary; understanding and using a range of language structures; improving their knowledge of print concepts; and we expose them to a range of concepts such as effective word choices, characterisation and so on. These are all secure foundations for both reading and writing. Texts invite us to talk, laugh, share, wonder and question. These meaningful interactions and discussions around texts promote and develop children's early language development.

At this stage, we will have pupils who struggle to write down their ideas (and not just at Key Stage 1!). However, many of these children have much to say and ideas aplenty; if they were able to put pen to paper, we might consider them to be some of our most advanced writers. We need to give these children opportunities to compose and produce meaningful outcomes. Without exposure to texts that challenge, how will they know what excellence looks like? Ultimately, a weakness in transcription skills should not be a barrier.

Text choice and concepts at Key Stage 1

As Bob says in Chapter 2, 'the appeal of the writing prises open the potential of the response. The teacher's knowledge and skill activates the process.' With this in mind, we need to think carefully about our text choices at Key Stage 1. As we are not asking children to read the words on the page (unless they are competent at this), we don't need to judge a text by its decodability. We may also be put off by challenging vocabulary, complex sentence structure, deeper meaning and ambiguity, yet this is exactly what we are striving for.

Very often, particularly at Key Stage 1, we look for texts that link to the rest of our curriculum rather than considering what they can offer in terms of our English curriculum. Quite rightly, children should share and discuss these books, but our desire to link English to other areas of the curriculum in the early stages of a topic may be at the expense of new learning through ambitious texts.

In addition to many of the points that Bob makes in Chapter 3, Key Stage 1 is no different. However, I am going to explore some distinct areas of thinking. One consideration for younger children may be how well the text can be linked to ideas, themes and content that they have encountered or are familiar with; the challenge will then be in the depth of the text and less so the content. An additional thought around text choice may well be: is this text relatable for my pupils? We can then move on to thinking about how the text can be used to teach, explore, develop and apply aspects of English.

Let us take the first verse of 'The Language of Cat' by Rachel Rooney:

Teach me the language of Cat;

the slow-motion blink, that crystal stare,

a tight-lipped purr and a wide-mouth hiss.

Let me walk with a saunter, nose in the air.

The experience the children bring of animals, plus linked work in school, can support their understanding of the content, allowing us to develop 'route-ways from curiosity to knowledge to familiarity and even to love'. The taster draft response below is from a Key Stage 1 child after encountering the first two lines of the poem. Whilst demonstrating an understanding of the content, it also shows her exploring and playing with language.

Teach me the language of Cat;

the slow-motion blink, that crystal stare,

the silver claws,

the who cares look.

The meow of joy,

a look of no.

A tail of yes,

the eye roll of maybe,

the happy look.

Olivia (Sparshalt Church of England Primary School)

Another example is *The Velveteen Rabbit* by Margery Williams, which explores many relatable ideas for Key Stage 1 – an exciting present, toys coming to life, a loved then forgotten toy – yet the text also displays a range of complexities.

So, does 'relatable' mean that the children should know about or have experienced something similar? Not necessarily. The example of pets may be applicable to many children (and would be a great starting point), whilst other content (such as a circus or a place they have little or no knowledge of) may be less so. However, we can investigate connections and pathways to support their understanding, perhaps through visits, wider reading, play and the curriculum. So, we scaffold the content in order to make it relatable and we are ambitious with the complexities of the text.

When we have a text in mind, we often think about linking it to a writing task. In the case of 'The Language of Cat', we might ask the children to write a poem about a cat. *The Velveteen Rabbit* might get us thinking about a story around a lost or abandoned toy. But how much deeper could we go with our thinking? What is that multilayered concept (see Chapter 9)? How about exploring word power within 'The Language of Cat' or characterisation in *The Velveteen Rabbit*? This opens up a wealth of writing opportunities for our 'wings to fly' (as described later in this chapter).

In summary, we search for routes in to access the text but also forge new pathways in English.

Getting started: sparking curiosity and access strategies

I would suggest, a few days in advance of the unit, planting a few seeds around something the children may encounter in the text. This isn't a hook per se; this is something far smaller and subtler designed to spark curiosity. We might think about a word or idea that the children encounter and start to familiarise them with it.

In 'The Language of Cat', Rooney explores the 'vanishing trick where dents in cushions appear'. Perhaps show, talk and speculate about a photo from someone's house of a dent in a cushion. What do we notice? What do we think? This isn't about looking for the correct answer(s), it is about interrogating different ideas. How many children will know what a dent is – you might like to spot a few! Another idea might be to introduce some link reading before the unit.

Consider the start of this poem by Robert Louis Stevenson:

The Little Land

When at home alone I sit
And am very tired of it,
I have just to shut my eyes
To go sailing through the skies –
To go sailing far away
To the pleasant Land of Play;
To the fairy land afar
Where the Little People are;
Where the clover-tops are trees,
And the rain-pools are the seas,
And the leaves, like little ships,
Sail about on tiny trips;
And above the Daisy tree
   Through the grasses,
High o'erhead the Bumble Bee
Hums and passes.

A few days (or weeks) in advance of the unit, we might link in some stories that explore size, fantasy and unusual characters, so the children build up some background to support their reading. We are enabling the material to be relatable. Fairy tales such as 'Jack and the Beanstalk' and 'Goldilocks' are great starting points, but why not include texts such as *Grandad's Secret Giant* by David Litchfield? We could also have some fun with changing the size of the furniture or objects in the room. How does it feel to use/be in the room?

Prior to and during the initial encounters with texts, the use of access strategies is key. It may be that more than one is needed. Whilst taster drafts give the children an opportunity to write and explore in the early stages, don't forget that this could include taster talk and taster role play. For example, after exploring the first six lines of 'The Little Land', we might ask the children to write a little bit about what the Land of Play might be like. Alternatively, they could create their own

Land of Play. You could use the construction area, role play, small world play, sand – the possibilities are endless. And then, of course, it is time to act their adventures out!

Utilising opportunities for play

In its non-statutory curriculum guidance for the early years foundation stage, the Department for Education (2020: 10) states:

> Effective pedagogy is a mix of different approaches. Children learn through play, by adults modelling, by observing each other, and through guided learning and direct teaching.
>
> Practitioners carefully organise enabling environments for high-quality play. Sometimes, they make time and space available for children to invent their own play. Sometimes, they join in to sensitively support and extend children's learning.

Play doesn't instantly stop when children enter Key Stage 1. To enable a smooth transition, deliberate decisions will be made around provision that are pertinent to the individual context of each school. But play is a fantastic opportunity for Opening Doors! Play can be embedded throughout the whole of the Opening Doors journey and applied to many of the strategies.

Coming back to Stevenson's 'The Little Land', we could consider:

- Sand and water play. What lands could we make with sand? Can we turn everyday objects into something different (e.g. leaves become ships)? Over time, we could leave out objects for the children to create what they want.

- Small world play: enacting the fantasy journey.

- Setting up a portal in our home corner. One half remains the home corner, but if they wish the children can travel (in their imaginations) through the portal to the Land of Play (or another land). What would be in the Land of Play? Part of the poem? Their own ideas?

- Links with forest school.

All of the above lends itself well to exploring the language in the poem. Whilst we can include items such as 'clovers' and 'grasses' from the poem within our play, well-planned interactions with adults during play is important. The adult might enact creatures 'marching by' or take ships on 'tiny trips' 'through the grasses', whilst modelling and supporting the use of new language.

We don't always need to completely change our role-play area to fit a text. We can enhance and develop existing provision. How about introducing a pet to link with 'The Language of Cat' or a toy cupboard that comes to life for *The Velveteen Rabbit*? Remember, adapting and enhancing play will add plenty of new opportunities for our pupils; we don't need to make big changes. A small change, a new object; less can be more!

Observe the children's talk during these activities: note the words and phrases they use to share with the class later and to enrich those deep discussions. You might join in by supporting and extending as needed.

Vocabulary

Part of the challenge (and excitement) for our younger children will be the vocabulary they encounter in the texts. It isn't just about knowing what the words mean, it is about how they may be used in a range of contexts: 'To have a commanding vocabulary is to master depth and breadth' (Lemov et al., 2016: 251).

How about introducing a vocabulary treasure board? As we explore and encounter descriptions within texts, we can talk with the children about words and phrases that we would consider to be real 'treasure' and add them to the board. We can also have some language play – for example, we can include the 'crystal stare' from 'The Language of Cat' but maybe add some stares of our own: the 'dark stare', the 'enquiring stare', the 'perplexed stare'.

Children need to encounter new words multiple times, so why not pick out a few words from our text or language play that we really want the children to know well? We will use these words deliberately in a range of contexts – for example, 'I'm perplexed as to why the Lego isn't tidy!' 'This question is perplexing.' Let all the adults know which words these are, so they can use them too within their daily encounters with your class.

Planning for success: extra steps and scaffolding (if needed)

True differentiation is a paradox. It is about having incredibly high expectations for every child. It's about regarding these as an entitlement. It is about offering demanding, concept rich, complex work. And the differentiation bit comes in through 'unpacking'. This means through high quality talk, questioning, checking for understanding, modelling, explaining. The most effective form of differentiation is through Dylan Wiliam's responsive teaching – preparing for the top and supporting pupils to get there, rather than deciding in advance which pupils will perform which tasks.

We must resist the temptation to dumb down. (Myatt, 2020b)

This is an important message: are we planning for failure or are we planning for success? Every child can be successful. We need to think about what the possible barriers might be for weaker readers and writers and how we could address these when planning, as opposed to deciding who can or can't do something in advance. You may be surprised!

Whilst decoding and encoding can be supported at the point of reading and writing within every unit (if necessary), we need to consider what other barriers there might be: cognitive overload, receptive and expressive language and so on. Rather than having lots of alternative activities up our sleeve, we require a few approaches and strategies that can be utilised across the Opening Doors approach.

In planning for success, you might like to consider some of these approaches as a starting point:

- Using visuals to support.

- Giving children options: do we think the cat is cross? Upset? Nervous?

- Open-ended starters and responses: *I feel … I think … I hear …*

- Think aloud 1and read aloud: modelling and scaffolding approaches.

❧ The gradual release of responsibility model.[3]

❧ Breaking the text down into smaller chunks.

❧ Charts and tables (see the following example).

Extract	Real	Not real	Illustration
Leaf	Leaf is real	It's not a ship	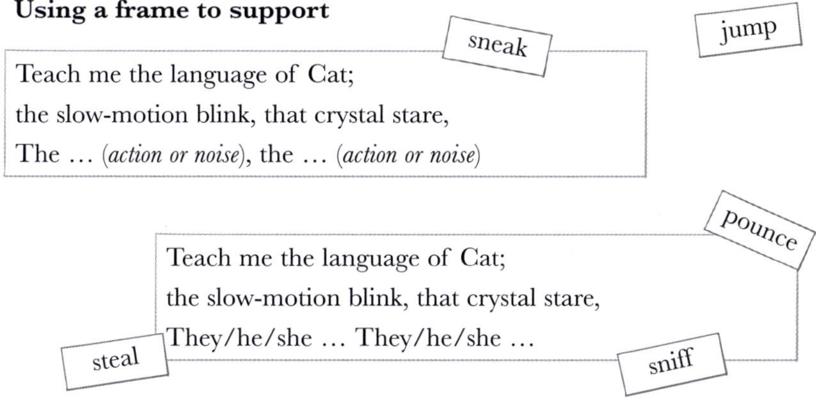
Fairy land			
Little People			
Clover-tops			
Rain-pools			
Daisy tree			

❧ A writing frame (see the following example): ensure that this is given to children who struggle to come up with ideas rather than children who struggle with the transcriptional elements of writing.

Using a frame to support

Teach me the language of Cat;

the slow-motion blink, that crystal stare,

The … (*action or noise*), the … (*action or noise*)

Teach me the language of Cat;

the slow-motion blink, that crystal stare,

They/he/she … They/he/she …

---

3   The gradual release of responsibility model is an instructional model whereby the teacher moves from taking all the responsibility for a task to a situation where the pupil assumes all the responsibility (see Duke and Pearson, 2002).

Phonics

Decoding and encoding are not a barrier for Opening Doors. The core programme for phonics will sit outside the Opening Doors approach, but it doesn't mean we can't make links or offer some additional learning.

I would suggest that the initial readings of the texts don't focus on decoding, as this isn't the core focus. Instead, the children can have an opportunity to listen and respond, if they are not yet reading independently. Following this, we can make links with what is taking place in phonics lessons. Perhaps try decoding and encoding words with grapheme–phoneme correspondences the children have been taught that appear in the text. Or how about spotting and noticing digraphs and trigraphs that the children are learning?[4]

However, we don't need to avoid words with grapheme–phoneme correspondence that doesn't match with what we have taught the children. Opportunities for incidental phonics can be explored too. Consider what might link and extend their current knowledge – what might be of particular interest? You might say: 'The word "stare" is interesting. We have learnt that the grapheme "air" can represent the /air/ phoneme, but in this word the grapheme "are" is representing /air/.' A quick explanation may well support widening and developing the children's phonic knowledge and making links with reading and writing. As Abigail Steel (2021: 11), phonics consultant and author of *Rocket Phonics*, comments: 'Teachers can also teach any letter-sound correspondences *incidentally* as required in phonics lessons and the wider curriculum.'

---

4   A digraph is two letters that represent one sound. A trigraph is three letters that represent one sound.

Using radial layouts with younger children: the big conversation

Chapter 10 explores radial layouts in considerable detail. We can use this approach with our less experienced readers to deepen their understanding and depth of response. However, we might wish to consider the following:

- Keeping the challenge of the central big question but putting the emphasis on the child as a reader. For example, the question, 'How does the poet show us what the cat is like?' becomes, 'How do you (the reader) know what the cat is like?'

- Presenting the approach as our 'big conversation'. The children get to be 'experts' who talk about writing for a time. In this way, we retain the challenge but make it more manageable.

- Following our initial big question/conversation, we break down into smaller conversations based around the need for scaffolding and support. When children need or wish to explore other conversations, they can join in more than one.

- To support the nature of a collaborative conversation, consider starting with a comment, not a question. This can be far less threatening and can open up the conversation: 'Let's look together at this word/phrase …' 'I wonder why the poet …?'

Have a look at the example on page 144 to see this in action.

I wonder why the poet uses a capital letter for Cat and Dog?
This tells me … I think …

I wonder what words and phrases show us that the cat is independent?
I spot … I notice …

Learn and recite the poem. Use your voice to convey the mood of the cat.

Big conversation starter (*all* children start with this), e.g. How do *you* know what the cat is like?

Compare other poems and prose about cats. How do these texts describe cats?

What does the poet think about the cat? How does she show this in her poem?
Why does she use the words 'teach me'?

I wonder what actions and sounds Dog makes? Spot words to describe Dog. How is Dog different to cat?
Dog … Cat …

Small group conversations
By need? By interest?
Join more than one
Comment and question
Adult as facilitator/prompter/provoker/challenger/modeller/scaffolder
Sentence starters: *I think … This tells me .. I wonder …*
Explore possibilities
Support and challenge

Look at some lines/phrases from the poem: 'tight-lipped purr', 'wide-mouth hiss', 'teach my ears the way to ignore', etc.
This tells me that … I wonder if … I felt … I thought …

Wings to fly

With the children now immersed in the text and having a deep understanding of a concept, it is time to give them a chance to apply this in their own writing. Traditionally, we work on a particular genre for a period of time, but what more could be on offer?

After exploring word power in 'The Language of Cat', pupils could:

❦ Write a new poem: 'The Language of Dog/Snake/Bird'.

❦ Write about an incident involving the cat in the poem.

❦ Describe the cat's (or another animal's) hideaway.

After exploring fantasy in 'The Little Land', pupils could:

❦ Create their own fantasy world: The Land of …

❦ Continue the adventure in the Land of Play.

❦ Turn an ordinary object into something unusual: 'The day the highlighter became a …'

All of these suggestions give the children an opportunity to express themselves and apply the concept in a piece of writing. The concept drives the writing rather than the genre.

And what of those who cannot yet put pen to paper? What do we do for them? Be careful of too much support or too many task completion activities. We must celebrate their outcomes too. We can scribe, record (audio or video) or present outcomes orally. Forcing children to write when they have little or no phonic knowledge and weak motor skills can result in disengagement – although we won't stop those who are keen!

Link reading

❦ 'Slowly' by James Reeves (Unit 3 in *Opening Doors to Quality Writing for Ages 6 to 9*)

❦ *Five Children and It* by Edith Nesbit (Unit 15 in *Opening Doors to Quality Writing for Ages 6 to 9*)

❦ 'Hurt No Living Thing' by Christina Rossetti (Unit 3 in *Opening Doors to a Richer English Curriculum for Ages 6 to 9*)

- ❦ 'Cat!' by Eleanor Farjeon (Unit 7 in *Opening Doors to a Richer English Curriculum for Ages 6 to 9*)
- ❦ 'The Frost, the Sun, and the Wind' (Russian folk tale translated by Charles Downing) (Unit 9 in *Opening Doors to a Richer English Curriculum for Ages 6 to 9*)

Key points on using Opening Doors at Key Stage 1

 Place a strong emphasis on *talk*.

 Share challenging and ambitious texts with children using *relatable* content.

 Develop opportunities for *play* throughout.

 Make *links with phonics*, and don't be afraid of a little incidental phonics teaching.

 Plan for *success*, not failure.

Case study: Challenging texts for Key Stage 1 pupils

Karen Smith, Christ Church Upper Armley Church of England Primary School, Leeds, West Yorkshire

Context

Our setting is an inner-city school situated on the outskirts of Leeds. With high levels of deprivation and many learners who speak English as an additional language, we consider ourselves both diverse and inclusive. Over the past four years, we have developed our whole-school curriculum with quality texts at the heart of everything we do. It was with this in mind that we decided to use the Opening Doors approach to teaching English, alongside the phased approach already embedded in the school, to ensure that we expose our children to a variety of challenging texts.

As the Year 2 teacher (of 6- and 7-year-olds), I have been able to experiment with different types of texts, using heritage texts such as *The Velveteen Rabbit* by Margery Williams, 'Daddy Fell Into the Pond' by Alfred Noyes, 'The Frost, the Sun, and the Wind' (a Russian folk tale) and 'The Island of the Nine Whirlpools' by Edith Nesbit. I have also experimented with *Treasure Island* by Robert Louis Stevenson as part of our topic 'The Seaside', using Opening Doors strategies.

Access for all – reading

In our setting, we use what we call a 'forensic approach' to teaching reading. This means that as well as teaching reading, using the Department for Education's (2021) guidance, we also study and read 'real books' in our daily guided reading sessions.

Within the session, we use reading for fluency and content domains to steer the teaching. Children use echo reading, closed reading, paired reading and choral reading to support fluency. As a consequence, all texts are accessible to all children, despite their prior reading experiences and reading attainment.

To ensure that all pupils are engaged with the more challenging texts recommended in the 'Opening Doors' books, we use our fluency strategies to read and learn the text on which we are working. This enables everyone to read and enjoy the text as they already have some knowledge of the words on the page.

Vocabulary/grammar

Whilst the children are immersed in the text, we also explore key vocabulary, phrases and grammar to ensure they have a good understanding of the content and can articulate their ideas. For example, the radial support questions on 'The Frost, the Sun, and the Wind' (Unit 9 of *Opening Doors to a Richer English Curriculum for Ages 6 to 9*), suggest that the children collect examples of dramatic direct speech and consider what makes it convincing. Other support questions include: 'Which vocabulary do you think creates personalities for the Frost, the Sun and the Wind? How? Can you write about the tone each personality is given in their speech?'

Writing

Once the children are familiar with the text, they will have the confidence to think about their writing. The children get very excited by the challenging vocabulary; rather than shying away from it, they want to use it and explore the contexts in which it can be used.

For example, here are some examples of pupils' work using the excellence criteria on personifying the forces of nature from the Opening Doors unit on 'The Frost, the Sun, and the Wind':

My Stormy Weather Report

Today I am feeling angry!

I will be thundering all day with a big angry face.

Don't forget to wear boots, coats, woolly gloves and an umbrella because my storm is very powerful.

I have noticed that when I thunder the people are scared of me.

By this evening the snow comes and gets rid of me but I will come again tomorrow.

Jasmine (this is a more able learner)

My Sunny Weather Report

Today I am feeling happy.

I am shining for the children.

You will need to wear sunglasses, a tee shirt and a hat.

I will be very hot today but in the evening I will be a beautiful sunset.

Felicity (this is a child with special educational needs and disabilities who we worked with one to one but shared her own ideas)

The Opening Doors approach to writing is exactly what we needed to support our English curriculum. The pupils are excited by the different texts and the challenges they bring. When children are disappointed that it's the end of the lesson, you know you are onto a winner!

ReSource 22

Chapter 12

Opening Doors to Non-Fiction

Angela Jenkins

To read is to fly: it is to soar to a point of vantage which gives a view over wide terrains of history, human variety, ideas, shared experiences and the fruits of many enquiries.

Anthony Grayling

A non-fiction book can be an aesthetic object … it can be a vehicle for a writer to talk directly to a reader about a subject about which they feel passionate … it can incite a reader to use their imagination or to empathize … it can have the same literary qualities that are appreciated in fiction, drama and poetry.

Nikki Gamble, *Exploring Children's Literature* (2019)

From recipes to hotel reviews, from match reports to museum and gallery guides, non-fiction is the most commonly encountered text in our everyday reading lives. Similarly, most of our time as authors is spent crafting emails, social media posts or perhaps, occasionally, a heartfelt note in a greetings card. Additionally, as children progress through education, the vast majority of reading and writing done in subjects beyond English will also be non-fiction.

Given its prominence in our lives beyond (and within) the classroom, sometimes non-fiction can get short shrift in English curriculum planning – perhaps confined to occasional non-fiction units with a weekly focus on different text types and littered with unconnected and uninspiring extracts and fabricated models thrown up by an internet search for 'explanation texts'. It is a bleak picture, but it doesn't have to be this way. Reading and writing non-fiction can be as engaging, purposeful and enjoyably challenging as fiction, drama and poetry within an ambitious English curriculum. Let us open the door.

What is non-fiction?

The term 'non-fiction' originates from the invention of the Dewey Decimal System for library classification in the nineteenth century and refers to anything that isn't fiction. That doesn't mean that non-fiction and fiction are opposites – they are not. There are many crossovers and common elements between fiction and non-fiction. If we think about historical novels, we recognise that authors will be sharing information about particular periods and settings. Many non-fiction texts will use narrative and literary devices more commonly associated with fiction, such as figurative language. As Nikki Gamble (2019: 227) explains: 'The balance of narrative and expository text in a non-fiction book will vary depending on subject, intended reader, or author's purpose.'

There is a huge range of non-fiction, including maps and atlases, news articles, travelogue, letters, reports and adverts, to name but a few. The breadth and variety are extensive. Given the potential for crossover with fiction, it is probably useful to think about non-fiction texts as existing on a continuum, trending more or less towards literary or informational text. The table on pages 154–155 maps a range of fiction and non-fiction texts according to mode, purpose and format. This table is a helpful visualisation of the extensive landscape of texts, and also draws our attention to the likelihood of writing having multiple purposes – note the arrows that stretch across the top row. Most non-fiction texts are hybrids; they don't conform solely to the conventions of any particular text type.

The drive for teaching non-fiction by text type possibly has its roots in the National Literacy Strategy (Department for Education and Skills, 1998), whose framework stipulated that children should be taught the tools to write in six different non-fiction formats (recount, report, instruction, explanation, persuasion and discussion). This was quickly picked up by education publishers, hence the proliferation of books written to include all the ingredients of the six text types. The legacy of the National Literacy Strategy and associated printed materials has contributed to non-fiction still being planned and taught in a paint-by-numbers way, despite the removal of any reference to text types in the current national curriculum programme of study for English (Department for Education, 2014).

A few words about disciplinary literacy

The rest of this chapter will focus on principles and strategies for teaching with teaching non-fiction in an ambitious English curriculum; however, it is important to recognise the value of selecting high-quality non-fiction texts across all subjects. When we are learning about key content in science or history, for example, the children are entitled to learn from the best resources. That means non-patronising texts written by experts in their field presented with accuracy and care. Occasionally, there will be appropriate times at which to make links from one area of the curriculum to another, but we should take care to maintain the integrity of the subject.

When it comes to writing, it makes sense for children to practise and apply what they have learnt about purpose, audience and form when composing texts relevant to the subject discipline – for example, when explaining the water cycle process in science. This kind of writing, which is rooted in the mode of communication commonly associated with a particular subject, provides a great opportunity for children to write authentic and purposeful texts.

It is worth making the important point here that a strong curriculum which builds knowledge about a range of different subjects empowers children as readers and writers in English and in every other curriculum subject. Knowledge and understanding of the world, its people and the relationships between them are essential for making sense of what we read and for deepening our comprehension. Equally, building knowledge about text structure, the author's craft and intertextuality nourishes the quality of children's writing. What this might look like in the English curriculum is explored in the rest of this chapter.

An overview of texts (Department of Education Western Australia, 2013: 4)

Tending towards literary text

Modes	MEDIA	Entertain	Recount	Socialise	PURPOSES Inquire
Written	Printed	Narrative Poem Song lyric Fairy tale Fable Myth	Biography Autobiography Diary Journal Retelling personal experience	Invitation Apology Message Note Personal correspondence	Survey Questionnaire
	Electronic	Joke		Chat room	
Spoken	Live	Joke Story Song lyric	Conversation	Greeting Apology Telephone conversation	Interview
	Electronic	Talking book Song lyric		Voicemail message	
Visual	Live	Play Theatre			
	Printed	Painting Photograph Cartoon	Picture book Photograph		
	Electronic	Television sitcom Film			

Tending towards informational text

Describe	Persuade	Explain	Instruct	FORMATS
Report	Exposition	Explanation	Directions	Magazine
Label	Menu	Affidavit	Timetable	Letter
Menu	Job application	Memo	Recipe	Book
Contents page	Editorial	Rules	Manual	Brochure
Index	Headlines	Policy	Invoice	Pamphlet
Glossary		Journal	List	Newspaper
		Timetable	Experiment	Chart
		Complaint	Summons	Journal
				CD-ROM
				Text message
				Email
				Card
Oral report	Debate	Oral explanation	Oral directions	Performance
	Discussion			Speech
	Talkback radio			Radio
	Song lyric			Television
				CD-ROM
				Clothing
				Tattoo
				Gesture
	Logo	Timeline	Road Sign	Button
	Advertisement	Graph		Flyer
	Catalogue	Table		Poster
		Flowchart		Magazine
Travel brochure		Documentary		CD-ROM
		News report		Web page

The Opening Doors approach to non-fiction in an ambitious English curriculum

What if we positioned non-fiction reading and writing as one of the golden threads running throughout our English curriculum? This thread would be woven into a rich tapestry of texts rather than a standalone swatch. This is turbocharged link reading! We are thinking here about clusters of texts, grouped to elucidate and exemplify key concepts in English, such as intertextuality and how writers use language and structure to convey information effectively.

Link reading can be based around a common theme or topic, perhaps providing multiple perspectives, or to illustrate variation in structure, vocabulary and grammar appropriate to purpose, audience and form. Non-fiction link reading can be used to build background knowledge so that understanding, analysis and interpretation of a central text is strengthened – for example, learning more about polar bears and threats to their habitat in order to access the deeper meaning of Hannah Gold's *The Last Bear*.

Non-fiction link reading can also build children's English subject knowledge of text structures, syntax, language and literary devices chosen for precision and effect. Research has demonstrated the success of using multiple texts to extend knowledge and widen vocabulary: 'By reading several texts that are connected by a unifying concept, pupils are able to benefit from a broader perspective and a deeper level of analysis (Cervetti et al., 2016)' (Horton et al., 2019: 107).

When teaching about form and genre, it is important to explore and analyse a variety of relevant texts as a means of grasping typical language features and structure, particularly for novice writers. Multiple models are vital.

Recognising and understanding the nuances of genre, the hybrid nature of non-fiction texts and learning about the author's craft, where choices are driven by purpose and audience in context (not just who they are but, more importantly, the effect we want to have on the reader), are key concepts for the study of non-fiction. This approach has been successfully implemented by colleagues at Rowner Junior School in Gosport, whose case study closes this chapter.

There should be points in our tapestry of texts when the non-fiction thread comes to the foreground and other times when it might form part of the background, the bigger picture. Thinking about the table of texts we considered earlier in this chapter, you will want to review whether your English curriculum includes a suitably challenging breadth and depth of non-fiction, and whether there is sufficient time and space given to literary non-fiction, such as biography, memoir, travelogue, editorials and specialist opinion pieces (for both reading and writing).

The example below focuses on memoir and takes Dara McAnulty's *Diary of a Young Naturalist* as the central text. It isn't a full unit (unlike those in the other 'Opening Doors' books) but seeks to illustrate how Opening Doors strategies might be applied when studying an ambitious non-fiction text.

Spotlight on literary non-fiction – memoir

Key concepts:

- The common components within narrative non-fiction, particularly when authors are writing about themselves, and personal experiences, such as memoir, autobiography, diaries and journals – for example, use of the first person, the selection of particular episodes to include and personal reflections that give meaning to experiences.

- Writers of non-fiction use language (words, phrases and figurative language) and structure (sentence and text level) in similar ways to fiction writers to effectively convey information and connect with the reader in a way that is specific to their context (what is important to them and what they are trying to achieve).

- Intertextuality is everywhere! Writers draw on their own reading when constructing texts, sometimes explicitly, sometimes implicitly.

In the award-winning *Diary of a Young Naturalist*, 15-year-old Dara 'chronicles the turning of my world, from spring to winter, at home, in the wild, in my head' (p. 17). Dara and his family live in Northern Ireland and they are all passionate about conservation and the natural world. Dara, his mother and his younger siblings (Lorcan and

Blathnaid) are autistic, so he shares his experiences through that lens, talking through his strengths and struggles.

It is a beautifully written memoir with important messages about caring for our planet and each other, but there are also many opportunities for readers to find 'common ground' with the author. As such, it is a text that can be a 'mirror', a 'window' and a 'sliding glass door' (Bishop, 1990). It is probably most suitable for upper Key Stage 2. It is entirely appropriate to read the whole text (or teachers may prefer to share an abridged version with children), lingering on and exploring particular passages in more depth.

Let us take a closer look at the entry for Saturday 26 May (pp. 55–56), in which Dara describes a visit to the seabird centre on Rathlin Island where his family are staying for a holiday. In the opening paragraph, Dara explains that there are lots of people at the centre: 'I build an imaginary suit of armour around myself and move forwards into the throng, senses popping like corn kernels.'

This is a rich fragment of text to explore *what* Dara is showing us about his feelings and *how* he is doing it. Together we can investigate the potential inferences from the imagery used ('suit of armour' and 'popping like corn') and word meaning and choice for 'throng'. We might include some wordplay and experimentation using 'throng' in different ways as a noun or a verb, and consider alternative synonyms such as 'crowd' or 'horde'. Why has Dara chosen 'throng'? What impact does it have on the reader?

Later in this entry for Saturday 26 May, we encounter a vivid and powerful description of the seabird centre from Dara's perspective:

When you first encounter the cliffs here during the breeding season, between May and July, everything gloriously slams into you at once. The not-quite pungent smell. The kaleidoscope of sounds. There are thousands of birds: guillemots, kittiwakes, razorbills, fulmars and puffins, all wheeling or diving, patrolling and protecting, sauntering over the shoulder of the stack. Mind-blowing. Magnificent. This is a place vibrating with survival and endurance. I feel tickled and almost hysterical, but must take it all in.

I try to focus on each species, starting with a fulmar, dozing and waiting, a queen on her throne, alone yet protected by the shadow of wings constantly flying past. She's like the Buddha in a trance, conserving energy, settling on the spot. Then the congregation of guillemots catches my eye, one heaving mass – safety in numbers – that completely cover the stack (the birds and the guano) … The kittiwake pair stick together on the cliffside and in the air. These ocean-faring nomads seem like the softest of gulls, but must be so hardy and tough to endure half a year out at sea – the young birds only return to land when they are two years old or more. (pp. 55–56)

There are many opportunities to teach and explore vocabulary and grammatical structures in context throughout the whole text and to consider how Dara manipulates them for effect – for example, using multi-clause sentences to give detail and portray contrasts: 'These ocean-faring nomads seem like the softest of gulls, but must be so hardy and tough to endure half a year out at sea – the young birds only return to land when they are two years old or more.' This is the ideal context in which to discuss the impact this structure has on the reader, using an authentic example from an authentic text, and for children to practise using the structure by imitating the pattern (Myhill et al., 2016). We may want to include taster draft writing tasks, such as inviting the children to write a short paragraph about an artefact (or person or place) they know well, incorporating some of the grammatical structures we have focused on.

Setting a challenging question (see Chapter 10) using a radial layout with appropriate scaffolds (such as supporting questions and visual images) provides a useful framework, enabling the children to move towards a deeper understanding and appreciation of how the author crafts such an evocative and engaging scene.

<table>
<tr>
<td>

Look closely at the first paragraph. What do you notice about the way Dara refers to different senses to help the reader imagine the scene?

</td>
<td>

Look closely at the description of the fulmar as 'a queen on her throne'. What impression does this create? What other words used in the description help to reinforce this impression?

</td>
</tr>
</table>

How well does the author craft an effective description of this episode and its impact on his mood and thinking?

<table>
<tr>
<td>

What clues are there to Dara's feelings? How do we know about his reactions to being at the seabird centre? How does he connect with the scene?

</td>
<td>

Greater depth

How does this episode contribute to the reader's understanding of Dara as the author? Are there connections we can make with other parts of the text or across the text as a whole?

Can we draw on our wider knowledge of memoir (and other texts) to inform our thinking?

</td>
</tr>
</table>

The importance of high-quality learning dialogues (see Chapter 8) is key for both establishing and analysing meaning at word and text level. The collaborative dialogue will help the pupils to identify the hallmarks of an effective response to the challenging question – the excellence criteria. This is likely to include:

❧ Exploration of language choice and its impact (powerful and precise noun/verb phrases such as 'gloriously slams' and the range of evocative verbs to describe the birds' behaviour, e.g. 'wheeling', 'diving', 'patrolling', 'protecting', 'dozing', 'sauntering').

❦ Reference to figurative language and imagery (e.g. 'kaleidoscope of sounds' and 'a queen on her throne').

❦ Appealing to the senses and how this links to emotion/feelings/ mood.

❦ Detailed subject knowledge of the birds, structured in an accessible and engaging way for non-experts (e.g. using multi-clause contrast sentences, comparisons with more familiar ideas or knowledge or other texts).

❦ Personal reflections – occasionally turning inwards to expose the impact on the author (metacognitive moments).

There are so many possibilities engendered by this text for meaningful, authentic writing tasks (wings to fly), but it seems to me that this ought to include an opportunity for the children themselves to write in a memoir style, perhaps about a memorable moment, place, person (or creature) and/or artefact (building on the taster draft). This is more focused than generic autobiography, which can sometimes feel too big and unwieldy, and it also means the children can select an episode to write about. It is important for teachers to know their class and to be mindful of potential sensitivities, but by giving children choice over the content of their memoir we are transferring authorial control to them.

Writing tasks that incorporate an element of choice, that allow children to write about content they know well and that matters to them mean they are more likely to craft effective texts, making writerly decisions that are driven by purpose, form and audience. Additionally, offering options around purpose, form and audience provides the opportunity for them to write with varying degrees of formality, choosing the appropriate register and making controlled choices about grammar and vocabulary. For example:

❦ An article for a special interest magazine (e.g. *National Geographic* or *110% Gaming*).

❦ An article for a general interest magazine (e.g. *The Week Junior* or *Aquila*).

❦ A guide to the local area, its wildlife and how to protect it (for children or families).

❦ A letter, speech or blog explaining why conservation (or any other passion) is important. This could be aimed at peers, the local community, school leaders or local leaders and written for a range of purposes – for example, to inform, influence opinion or persuade them to act.

As we have already established, link reading is vital in order to read with depth and to write effectively. There are so many great options to choose from when creating a cluster of texts to accompany the study of *Diary of a Young Naturalist*. Some of these may include other examples of the memoir genre and/or a neurodiverse authorial/character perspective, and/or the theme of difference and inclusion, and/or dealing with important environmental concerns. Below are just a few suggestions which pick up on the theme of conservation action.

Fiction	Non-fiction	Picture books	Poetry
The Last Bear or *The Lost Whale* by Hannah Gold, illustrated by Levi Pinfold) *Julia and the Shark* by Kiran Millwood Hargrave, illustrated by Tom de Freston *The Last Wild* by Piers Torday	*The Biggest Footprint* by Rob Sears and Tom Sears *Rewilding* by David A. Steen, illustrated by Chiara Fedele *Wild Child* by Dara McAnulty, illustrated by Barry Falls *Many* by Nicola Davies, illustrated by Emily Sutton	*The Great Kapok Tree* by Lynne Cherry *The Promise* by Nicola Davies, illustrated by Laura Carlin *This Morning I Met a Whale* by Michael Morpurgo, illustrated by Christian Birmingham	*A Year of Nature Poems* by Joseph Coelho, illustrated by Kelly L. Judd *Cherry Moon* or *When Poems Fall from the Sky* by Zaro Weil , illustrated by Junli Song *Dark Sky Park* by Philip Gross, illustrated by Jesse Hodgson

Fiction	Non-fiction	Picture books	Poetry
October, October or *Birdsong* by Katya Balen, illustrated by Richard Johnson	Biographies, speeches and articles from other conservation activists such as Greta Thunberg and Severn Cullis-Suzuki. Haig and Lennon's *Talking History* (2022) includes speeches from both.		'Give and Take' by Roger McGough 'Autumn Gilt' or 'Two Seasons' by Valerie Bloom Works from Romantic poets such as John Keats ('To Autumn') and William Wordsworth ('I Wandered Lonely as a Cloud') celebrate the majesty of the natural world.

Sourcing and selecting high-quality, diverse and authentic non-fiction texts is a joy! Book award shortlists (such as the UK Literacy Association) and recommendations from credible organisations (such as BookTrust, CLPE and the National Literacy Trust) are useful sources. The Federation of Children's Book Groups facilitates an annual celebration, National Non-Fiction November, including themed booklists, book reviews and competitions. Remember that you can celebrate non-fiction all year round though!

Link reading

For more Opening Doors non-fiction units, see:

- *The American Woman's Home* by Catherine E. Beecher and Harriet Beecher Stowe (Unit 11 in *Opening Doors to a Richer English Curriculum for Ages 6 to 9*)

- *The Story of the Blue Planet* by Andri Snær Magnason (Unit 15 in *Opening Doors to a Richer English Curriculum for Ages 6 to 9*)

- Fake News – In Search of the Truth (Unit 15 in *Opening Doors to a Richer English Curriculum for Ages 10 to 13*)

Key points on using non-fiction

Consider the full range of non-fiction reading and writing when exploring the role it plays in your English curriculum. Be ambitious about *breadth and depth*, and recognise the *hybrid nature of non-fiction* and the nuances of genre. Avoid too much talk of text type.

Choose *high-quality texts* that are fit for purpose. Remember that some non-fiction, like advertising, becomes out of date quickly. Ensure that texts are *representative* of a range of realities.

Weave non-fiction reading and writing throughout the English curriculum wherever possible. Design *meaningful and authentic writing tasks* which include opportunities for children to exercise choice, write about what they know and demonstrate authorial control.

Plan for children to encounter *clusters of texts* through link reading. Texts will fulfil a range of purposes such as building background knowledge, strengthening understanding of an author's craft and exploring how different writers deal with common themes and conventions. Non-fiction link reading can be positioned in the background and in the foreground.

 Shine a light on *literary non-fiction* in English. Ensure there is sufficient focus in the curriculum on reading *whole texts as well as extracts*, including biographical and autobiographical writing, essays, articles and opinion pieces, reviews, reports and other evaluative writing.

Case study: Developing non-fiction

Emily Weaver, Rowner Junior School, Gosport, Hampshire

At Rowner Junior School, we aim to weave rich tapestries of texts that teach concepts, not genre features; pupils are exposed to and actively explore a broader diet of literature. Over the last five years, we have built a curriculum that combines whole texts and extracts. Writers of heritage works sit alongside the likes of Andri Snær Magnason, Benjamin Zephaniah and Zlata Filipović. We are always expanding the canon of authors we study to immerse pupils in a wider range of cultures and history. Whilst this journey felt logical and more familiar for narratives and poetry, non-fiction presented a different kind of challenge. Letting go of genre as a driving force for teaching non-fiction has opened up possibilities which previously felt more limited and made learning seem shallow.

'Big questions' sit at the heart of our English curriculum, so creating these for non-fiction was our original starting point. The design of a thoughtful question to sit centre stage enables high pitch but also appropriate access: it allows room at the top to ensure stretch and for pupils to demonstrate 'assured and conscious control' during the writing process (Standards and Testing Agency, 2018: 5). Alongside this, we aim to ensure that learners have absolute clarity on the purpose and impact they wish to have on their audience. By looking at a text through the focus of a big question, learners are able to build a toolkit of how an author has achieved a particular effect and impacted on the audience; we learn from being engaged with a range of high-quality examples.

When starting our non-fiction journey, we soon realised that there is a blurred line between non-fiction and fiction. We found that we could classify writing into four main strands: non-fiction to inform, non-fiction in a more traditional sense, fictitious non-fiction and literary non-fiction. We wanted to be able to immerse our children in all of these texts. In order to understand the purpose, we need to look at the intended impact of a non-fiction text, and this has moved us away from the constraints of genre.

In Year 4, pupils study Hannah Gold's novel *The Last Bear*, which raises the issues of climate change and conservation. This was used as a basis for writing a persuasive text. Historically, we would have explored this as a stand alone text, looked at examples of speeches and then written our own. This time round, a tapestry of both fiction and non-fiction allowed our learners to develop vocabulary, background knowledge, genre, purpose – the list goes on.

The big question provided clarity about what to look for and focus on when encountering a range of texts, but it also supported learners in building a toolkit for when it came to writing their own speeches. In this example, the question was: 'How can we write to inform and convince those who are disconnected from the impact of their actions to change?' The impact on the audience was made explicitly clear: the reader is informed of the pressing issues facing the environment but also feels empowered to change their own behaviour (with a sense of urgency). This solid foundation and careful consideration of the learning journey laid the path to high-quality written outcomes.

What did the tapestry look like? Learners were exposed to the plight of the Arctic and global heating through different forms, including *National Geographic* interviews with those working in the Arctic, NASA reports on greenhouse gases, the author's notes from the novel (outlining the inspiration for the story of *The Last Bear*) and blogs of modern-day explorers. Thus, building background knowledge for speech writers to draw upon.

When it came to learning about the emotions required to persuade, we turned to other inspiration. Greta Thunberg was a relatable example for our learners – but how best to present her story? This came in a range of texts from across the four strands mentioned above: the picture book *Greta and the Giants* by Zoë Tucker; two different versions of her life story – *Little People, Big Dreams: Greta Thunberg* by Maria Isabel Sánchez Vegara and *Greta's Story: The Schoolgirl Who Went on Strike to Save the Planet* by Valentina Camerini; finally, copies of Greta's famous 2019 speech to the World Economic Forum at Davos, 'Our House is on Fire', and her open letter to EU leaders.[1]

This wide range of exposure to vastly different presentations and interpretations led to our learners gathering an invaluable assemblage of knowledge to be able to both inform and persuade with urgency. This gave them the power to be able to convince someone that they needed to personally change their actions.

We recently revisited the unit with our learners, presenting them with their books from the previous year and asking them if they could remember the processes they had been through as writers. Without fail, they could all articulate the reasons behind the choices they had made and could explain to visiting English leaders how certain decisions had impacted the intended audience. This really showed that the Opening Doors approach, when applied to non-fiction, had created learning that had stuck, and stuck firmly.

---

1   See https://climateemergencyeu.org.

Resource 24

ADLESTROP

Chapter 13

Teaching Poetry

Bob Cox

Imagine what you are writing about. See it and live it. Do not think it up laboriously, as if you were working out mental arithmetic. Just look at it, touch it, smell it, listen to it, turn yourself into it. When you do this, the words look after themselves, like magic.

Ted Hughes, *Poetry in the Making* (1967)

Why would the teaching of poetry merit a separate chapter when considering ambitious English? In many ways, the aim is to place poetry at the heart of the English curriculum, so the principles and strategies we explore in this book of course apply to poetry.

However, there are distinctive challenges in planning for and exploring poetry with primary-age children. These revolve around the lack of confidence some teachers have in using, modelling and mapping poetry throughout the curriculum, especially as the texts get more complex throughout the phase.

The following key questions often arise on my travels: is poetry too difficult to teach? Can it be taught at all? Should we just focus on recital and exploration instead? I wonder whether primary teachers' experiences of poetry have been limited or truncated, or whether some teachers just find poetic styles unfamiliar and baffling. Does this mean that fun rhymes, limericks and nonsense poetry are included in the English curriculum more often than complex poetry, rap, sonnets, epics or narrative ballads?

The reasons behind the dearth of poetry in the primary curriculum have been explored by Dawn Robertson (2020) in her excellent article for *Primary Matters*. She investigates why poetry has got such a bad reputation with some teachers and offers resources and ideas on how to get inspired. Julie Blake's (2019) dissertation on the use of poetry at GCSE level is also relevant to building a rationale for poetry in primary schools. Her evidence-led argument for exploring long-term debates about poetry in education is excellent.

So, what is the added value of poetry?

Poetry is music: it offers telling phrases, opportunities to learn and recite, profound moments and great fun. The virtuosity of poetry creates a context for crafting, questioning and wondering, which can have a huge impact on the whole-school curriculum. Through poetry, great thinking and debating can begin, new vocabulary can be found and a world of famous writers can develop. It offers a licence to challenge the so-called rules of grammar and create all kinds of word symphonies. It is freedom from straitjackets!

The range is endless: from narrative ballads in traditional rhythms by Tennyson, dialect forms from Valerie Bloom, rap poetry from Karl Nova to clever and funny wordplay from performance poets like Joshua Seigal or A. F. Harrold. Through poetry, the difference a comma can make to reading and meaning or a change of meter to the pronunciation and impact of a final line will become clearer to your pupils. Through poetry, emotions are articulated or hilarious episodes described. The music and prosody of poetry is a teacher's gift for the development of fluency, echo reading and recitation, which deepens comprehension, familiarity and the love of words.

The more I encounter great poetry teaching, the more cross-curricular it becomes, not just at the heart of English but also in the wider and deeper elements of the primary curriculum: global concerns, well-being, family, religion, peace and war. Poets explore the beating heart of mankind, past and present.

Like me, you will have met people who are left cold by poetry; I confess that I was late to it myself. It was only when I began teaching poetry – and realised how many times I needed to feel the flow of the words in and out of me – that I started to deepen my responses to the lyricism of the rhythm and meaning. Yet, how many people do you know who reach for poetry on sad occasions like funerals and happy ones like weddings? There is usually a chorus of approval that only a poem can match the tenor of both those sharply contrasting occasions. The reading of a poem on days like these pierces the awareness and consciousness of each listener, like a transmitter reaching many different receivers.

No poem sits in the world separate from the other artistic things we do. When we read a poem, our reaction to it is partly based on these things: the songs, films, paintings and TV programmes that we have seen or heard. (Rosen, 2016: 89)

A poetry immersion

So, how can our approaches to poetry tackle some of the deep-rooted reservations that may be filtering through your staff meetings? And if you and your staff are already confident with poetry, how can Opening Doors approaches help you be even more ambitious?

A starting point for ensuring the inclusion of poetry that teachers can access and make use of in units of work is the stock cupboard itself! To ignite more metacognitive talk in your staffroom book debates, try including well-known poets like Emily Dickinson or Ted Hughes in conjunction with contemporary poets like Valerie Bloom, Joseph Coelho, Philip Gross, Sue Hardy-Dawson, Brian Moses, Michael Rosen or Kate Wakeling. Consider traditional anthologies that can still teach children much about wordplay, rhythm, meaning and creativity, like James Reeves' *Complete Poems for Children*, alongside a recent anthology, like *The Proper Way to Meet a Hedgehog*, edited by Paul B. Janeczko.

Interestingly, the legacy of the era of the primary poetry anthology can be seen in the relaxed way teachers use poems like Walter de la Mare's 'The Listeners', Tennyson's 'The Lady of Shalott' or Alfred Noyes' 'The Highwayman'. I realised some time ago that it isn't the language and literary challenge of ambitious poetry that deters teachers but lack of familiarisation. Teachers who have internalised their own favourites from childhood and training seem better equipped to relish the discovery of new texts. We have seen many teachers use the 'Opening Doors' series and, of course, other superb resources, like those curated and written by the CLPE, to plan for poetry in exciting ways.

Planning for poetry

Reflect on the following points when including top-quality poetry in your English curriculum:

- ❦ Have you included the teaching of aspects of poetry – like structure, rhythm or the use of metaphor – which get progressively harder during each key stage? Have you considered a focus on, for example, sonnets, narratives, nonsense verse or haiku?

- ❦ Are there examples of poetry in a range of styles displayed around the school?

- ❦ Are your budding poets getting the chance to have their writing appear on a website or read out loud?

- ❦ Are you encouraging a community of poets?

- ❦ Are challenging poems included in your link reading selections (see Chapter 6)?

- ❦ Are you teaching concepts rather than 'doing' a poem? This supports the mindset that leads, for example, to the teaching of metaphor and meaning across texts rather than listing metaphors in one poem for its own sake.

Surround not just the pupils but also your colleagues with poem after poem! I once asked each teacher to contribute their favourite poem to a display and explain why they had chosen it, but I also asked them to choose a new poem that they thought might become a favourite in time. The talk arising from this activity generated very productive and sometimes emotional comments on a poem's impact. You can also include the reading of poetry in story-time selections. Choose poems that are more readily accessible but have ample scope for reading aloud with all sorts of voices.

How to access more advanced poems

I would like now to take the kind of risk I am always recommending to teachers by demonstrating how a poem that originally left me emotionless and unresponsive, 'Adlestrop' by Edward Thomas, can be explored in a creative way. It is a poem I now love!

I have been using 'Adlestrop' in my sessions with teachers who are unfamiliar with it to think through ways of applying Opening Doors principles and strategies. My fondness for the poem has grown over time through many rereadings, but could it be used with primary pupils? It regularly crops up in old anthologies, along with poets like Emily Dickinson, John Masefield, Edward Lowbury, Christina Rossetti, Walter de la Mare and T. S. Eliot. Our schools are finding that, when grouped around concepts, carefully selected poems from the past can coexist in very rich ways with poets writing for children (and adults) successfully now. There is a list of poems and poets which may help you at https://searchingforexcellence.co.uk/poetry-resources.

I hope you can follow this sequence through to the end and that 'Adlestrop' starts to mean something special to you too. You can adapt the strategies described here for any poem, especially one with challenging language or notions, so that all pupils can access and enjoy it.

'Adlestrop' by Edward Thomas

https://www.poetryfoundation.org/poems/53744/adlestrop

Here is a potential pathway for the teaching of a complex poem – not a full unit but some key pointers.

Access

Stepping stone 1

Do *not* read out the full poem but just quote the first line: 'Yes. I remember Adlestrop—'

- What place do you remember?
- Why is it important? Can you describe the place?
- What kind of place might Adlestrop be? Why?
- Why might the poem begin with a single assertive 'Yes'?

You are asking for an exploration of sounds and associations as well as the emotional power of a memory.

Stepping stone 2

Feed your pupils these few lines from the second stanza:

The steam hissed. Someone cleared his throat.

No one left and no one came

On the bare platform. What I saw

Was Adlestrop—only the name

- ❦ What happens in this stanza? What sounds are there? Is the hissing relevant to the meaning? Can you find a connection across the images?

- ❦ Write a taster draft about something seen from a train window that builds an atmosphere of expectation. Imitate Edward Thomas' style.

All your explanations and advice can now focus around the concept of senses and sounds in a poem. Teaching about this becomes the rationale underscoring the lessons.

Stepping stone 3

Read out the first three stanzas in full:

Yes. I remember Adlestrop—

The name, because one afternoon

Of heat the express-train drew up there

Unwontedly. It was late June.

The steam hissed. Someone cleared his throat.

No one left and no one came

On the bare platform. What I saw

Was Adlestrop—only the name

And willows, willow-herb, and grass,
And meadowsweet, and haycocks dry,
No whit less still and lonely fair
Than the high cloudlets in the sky.

❦ Write up to five words which sum up the atmosphere of the poem.

❦ Predict the final stanza.

❦ Write a taster draft poem which could include: a place with an unusual name, images of quiet, silence with occasional noises, use of punctuation like dashes and semicolons to influence reading for meaning. Keep to a word or time limit.

Feedback and advice

The children's comprehension and appreciation of the poem has been connecting like a cognitive field of learning, a jigsaw that slowly pieces together. Those finding it hardest will have been supported by:

❦ The stepping stones to knowledge acquisition.

❦ The time taken with learning dialogues.

❦ The brevity of a taster draft which gives scope for all abilities.

❦ Your clear explanations.

❦ The slow reveal, so that the harder stanza three comes only when other aspects of the poem have already been explored.

❦ Reading aloud, particularly by you, meaning that the short sentence, 'It was late June', can be read after a mini pause. Your emphasis will hugely support access to the poem. Later, the pupils can all recite at least parts of the poem and echo the lines they enjoy.

Refer to the powerful Ted Hughes quote at the start of this chapter from one of the most famous books written about poetry. Now is the time when the brain can flow, as Hughes advises. Enough has now been learnt about the quality of the poem and from all kinds of prior reading experiences to start crafting!

Quality text to quality writing

Ask the children to write a final stanza which echoes and rings in the imagination rather than creating a thumping finale incongruent with the first three stanzas. Compare their writing with the blackbird which has been singing through readers' minds since 1917 – but don't reveal it until after they have read out their own drafts.

And for that minute a blackbird sang

Close by, and round him, mistier,

Farther and farther, all the birds

Of Oxfordshire and Gloucestershire.

Hopefully, you been able to teach them that a poem can have a reflective, echoing ending which isn't always overt or in the face.

These are just some brief outline ideas, and nothing like the 80 full units in the book series, but I am keen to enthuse you to try a poem like this with your pupils – adding your own ideas, of course. The vocabulary in 'Adlestrop' isn't hard, but the connotations and the distillation of that minute when the blackbird sings into a moment is subtle for a reader. Edward Thomas was killed in the First World War, so this poem also provides a counterpoint to society at that time. It was based on a railway journey Thomas took on 24 June 1914, before the war began.

Why not ask for silence for a minute in class? Time it. Play the blackbird singing from the following link for those sixty seconds: https://www.youtube.com/watch?v=EB1lgjg9e4Y.   What thoughts fill the time for your pupils?

It is now time to link quality text to quality writing in the way our schools enjoy the most (see Chapter 4), linking the language development from their thinking about senses to the emotional engagement felt from the birdsong and the silence.

Ask your pupils to write a full poem featuring sights, sounds and associated images but little action. This will be a poem in which nothing happens yet everything happens.

I now know that I originally thought 'Adlestrop' was dull because I hadn't read enough poetry and I didn't understand the metaphorical birdsong or what Thomas was implying between the lines. You are the conduit through which poets' words live on. Primary pupils have the inclination to reach for new styles and meaning, *if* you act as their guide across new territory. You can turn an order of words, a style, or a mystery previously beguiling to your pupils into new curiosities to treasure.

You could say that including classic and ambitious poetry in the primary phase is a kind of social justice, an entitlement for all, and it will certainly make the Key Stage 3 stepping stones a lot more manageable.

Link reading

- *Stars with Flaming Tails* by Valerie Bloom
- *If I Were Other Than Myself* by Sue Hardy-Dawson
- *101 Poems for Children* edited by Carol Ann Duffy
- *Complete Poems for Children* by James Reeves

Each of the five 'Opening Doors' books contains poetry units, but try looking at these in particular:

- 'The Inchcape Rock' by Robert Southey (Unit 3 in *Opening Doors to Famous Poetry and Prose*)
- 'Snake' by Emily Dickinson (Unit 6 in *Opening Doors to Famous Poetry and Prose*)
- 'The New Vestments' by Edward Lear (Unit 1 in *Opening Doors to Quality Writing for Ages 6 to 9*)

- ❦ 'Lonely Street' by Francisco López Merino (Unit 8 in *Opening Doors to Quality Writing for Ages 6 to 9*)

- ❦ 'Mementos' by Charlotte Brontë (Unit 9 in *Opening Doors to Quality Writing for Ages 10 to 13*)

- ❦ 'A Garden at Night' by James Reeves (Unit 13 in *Opening Doors to Quality Writing for Ages 10 to 13*)

- ❦ 'Hurt No Living Thing' by Christina Rossetti (Unit 3 in *Opening Doors to a Richer English Curriculum for Ages 6 to 9*)

- ❦ 'Green Candles' by Humbert Wolfe (Unit 5 in *Opening Doors to a Richer English Curriculum for Ages 6 to 9*)

- ❦ 'The Door' by Miroslav Holub (Unit 1 in *Opening Doors to a Richer English Curriculum for Ages 10 to 13*)

- ❦ 'Cold Mountain' by Han-Shan (Unit 4 in *Opening Doors to a Richer English Curriculum for Ages 10 to 13*)

Key points on teaching poetry

Poetry should be *an integral part* of a primary English curriculum, not a bolt-on project day.

Ensure a *progression route* for poetry through Key Stages 1 and 2 and into 3; concepts can be repeated but texts and objectives get harder.

Include lots of poetry in your link reading selections, which can be planned for year by year, getting progressively harder. *Intertextuality is then facilitated* by the systems you have in place.

Teachers and pupils *build knowledge about poetry* by being surrounded by poems and opportunities to read, recite, browse and reflect.

The more challenging the poem, *the more the teacher is needed to find specific strategies and stages* through which to bring subtle meaning and craft alive.

Appreciating an ambitious poem is a journey where *comprehension grows through new knowledge awareness*. Take it step by step. Imagine you are crossing a river on stepping stones. Don't let the memory banks get flooded and take in the view at each stone.

Reading poetry for pleasure is as much a part of *reading aloud and fluency work* as reading stories.

Aim for your pupils to go to secondary school equipped with a *deep reading background in a range of poetry* and with knowledge of many poets, past and present and from across the globe.

Case study: Poetry at the heart of the curriculum

Sonia Thompson, St Matthew's Church of England Primary School, Birmingham

At St Matthew's, we have a deep love for both poetry and its performance. Alongside prose and non-fiction, it takes its place at the heart of our reading and writing curriculum. We read and perform both classics and contemporary poems and have had author visits from Karl Nova, Joseph Coelho and Michael Rosen. We have also taken part in and won the Centre for Literacy in Primary Poetry Award (CLiPPA) Shadowing Scheme.

Not only do we relish the opportunities poetry offers us to savour its delights, but also the privilege it allows us to deepen our children's hinterland – from finding out about the lives of poets to discussing their themes and effects, the gamut of emotions they can evoke and, of course, uncovering ambitious vocabulary. Our teachers have enabled the children to build a knowledge bank of poets and their wonderful words and narratives.

Deliberate curriculum sequencing means that poetry leads us off each term. This enables reading aloud, learning poetry by heart and literary analysis to permeate every classroom. Opening Doors approaches have deftly supported our teachers to open doors to an ethic of excellence through diverse and progressively more ambitious poetry and poets across the school. For example, we use James Reeves' 'The Hippocrump' in Year 2, Christina Rossetti's 'What is Pink?' in Year 3 and Paul Laurence Dunbar's 'Sympathy' in Year 6.

The impact has been exciting and wide-ranging. Alongside the obvious benefits for the children, Opening Doors has offered our teachers the chance to deepen their poetry subject knowledge. Through accessing and applying the link reading to their planning and teaching, teachers' growing confidence in teaching poetry has led to a tangible improvement in their appreciation of poetry as well as an improvement in the quality of pupils' poetry writing. Children regularly choose poetry books to read for pleasure, and are comfortable and confident when reciting poetry in class assemblies and whole-school musical performances.

Most recently, our Year 6 'Sympathy' poems have been particularly impactful and demonstrate the power of Opening Doors teaching sequences. It inspired our young writers to express themselves richly through their poems, using quality poetry as a model.

For me, what Opening Doors has ultimately offered St Matthew's is the opportunity to cement our appreciation of ambitious poetry and make our love of poetry even more palpable and powerful.

End note

In a long, fulfilling and challenging career in education, I have travelled the length and breadth of the UK and presented ideas in many other countries. I have taught for twenty-three years and supported over 500 schools directly and thousands indirectly through the 'Opening Doors' books for almost the same amount of time. It is a huge privilege.

No doubt, debate will continue around methodology, pedagogy, the use of ICT, the generalisability of evidence, behaviour management, creativity and so on. When governments change, the angle of emphasis tends to alter too. Yet I, and all my co-authors, have found that there is a coherent pattern to the most exciting aspects of school improvement and the deepening of learning and knowledge: the quality of leadership and the excellence of the teachers.

Schools thrive when there is a self-reflective culture and a metacognitive ethos. These are the schools where the staff ask questions and expect the pupils to ask questions too. Teachers who grow to love and need challenge and ambition as a norm often feel less stressed in these contexts, not more. We have seen them take charge of curriculum development and use CPD and books like this one to feed action plans and personal enthusiasms. Learning and new knowledge is then acquired more intrinsically. It is relished rather than resisted. Teachers develop more confidence and resilience with an impulse to pitch high and include every pupil becoming a regular classroom habit. Teachers develop confidence as well as resilience and an impulse towards excellence rather than mediocrity.

At the heart of social justice is equity and excellence for all. Our schools have worked with us on this book to provide some of the fine-tuning that may stimulate a move towards schools having more autonomy in preparing and delivering a curriculum that is tailored to need. The most important thing I have learnt in a long career is that it is the quality of the teacher that makes the difference – and growing that quality is a head teacher's number one goal because the rest will follow.

All the 'Opening Doors' authors hope you will integrate the principles and strategies explored in this book into your own ways of working to make an even deeper impact on the teaching of English in your classroom. We hope it helps you to grow your own vision for literacy through literature – which is the entitlement of every pupil.

Bibliography

Primary sources

Agard, John (2003). 'Clockwise', in *Hello H₂O*. London: Hodder & Stoughton.

Agee, John (2019). *The Wall in the Middle of the Book*. London: Scallywag Press.

Aiken, Joan (2012 [1962]). *The Wolves of Willoughby Chase*. London: Random House.

Alcott, Louisa May (2018 [1868]). *Little Women and Good Wives*. Ware: Wordsworth Editions.

Baum, L. Frank (1993 [1900]). *The Wizard of Oz*. Ware: Wordsworth Editions.

Balen, Katya (2020). *October, October*. London: Bloomsbury.

Balen, Katya (2022). *Birdsong*, ill. Richard Johnson. Edinburgh: Barrington Stoke.

Bilan, Jasbinder (2019). *Asha and the Spirit Bird*. Frome: Chicken House.

Bilan, Jasbinder (2020). *Tamarind and the Star of Ishta*. Frome: Chicken House.

Bloom, Valerie (2000a). 'Autumn Gilt', in *Let Me Touch the Sky*. London: Macmillan.

Bloom, Valerie (2000b). 'Time', in *The World is Sweet*. London: Bloomsbury.

Bloom, Valerie (2000c). 'Two Seasons', in *The World is Sweet*. London: Bloomsbury.

Bloom, Valerie (2009). 'Frost', in *Hot Like Fire and Other Poems*. London: Bloomsbury.

Bloom, Valerie (2021). *Stars with Flaming Tails*. Hereford: Otter-Barry Books.

Brahmachari, Sita (2019). *Where the River Runs Gold*. London: Hodder & Stoughton.

Brand, Dionne (2006 [1979]). 'Wind', in *Earth Magic*. Toronto: Kids Can Press.

Brontë, Anne (1997 [1846]). 'Lines Composed in a Wood on a Windy Day', in *The Brontës*. London: Everyman's Poetry.

Brontë, Charlotte (1921). 'Speak of the North!', in John C. Squire (ed.), *A Book of Women's Verse*. Oxford: Clarendon Press. Available at: https://www.bartleby.com/291/118.html.

Brontë, Emily (1995 [1847]). *Wuthering Heights*. Oxford: Oxford World Classics.

Camerini, Valentina (2019). *Greta's Story: The Schoolgirl Who Went on Strike to Save the Planet*, ill. Veronica Carratello, tr. Moreno Giovannoni. London: Simon & Schuster.

Carroll, Lewis (1993 [1865/1871]). *Alice's Adventures in Wonderland and Through the Looking-Glass*. Ware: Wordsworth Editions.

Cherry, Lynne (2000). *The Great Kapok Tree: A Tale of the Amazon Rainforest*. London: Harcourt Brace.

Coelho, Joseph (2016). 'Wind', in *Overheard in a Tower Block*. Hereford: Otter-Barry Books.

Coelho, Joseph (2020). *A Year of Nature Poems*, ill. Kelly L. Judd. London: Wide Eyed Editions.

Coleridge, Samuel Taylor (1996 [1798]). *The Rime of the Ancient Mariner and Other Classic Stories in Verse*. London: Penguin.

Collins, Wilkie (1974 [1868]). *The Woman in White*. Harmondsworth: Penguin.

Collodi, Carlo (1995 [1883]). *Pinocchio*. Ware: Wordsworth Editions.

Conan Doyle, Arthur (1999 [1901]). 'The Hound of the Baskervilles', in *The Hound of the Baskervilles and The Valley of Fear*. Ware: Wordsworth Editions.

Cook, Eliza (2018). 'Song of Old Time', in Susannah Herbert (ed.), *Poetry for a Change: National Poetry Day Anthology*. Hereford: Otter-Barry Books.

Davies, Nicola (2013). *The Promise*, ill. Laura Carlin. London: Walker Books.

Davies, Nicola (2020). *Many: The Diversity of Life on Earth*, ill. Emily Sutton. Somerville, MA: Candlewick Press.

Davies, William H. (1911). 'Leisure', in *Songs of Joy and Others*. New York: University of California Libraries.

de la Mare, Walter (1979 [1912]). 'The Listeners', in *Walter de la Mare: Collected Poems*. London: Faber & Faber.

de Saint-Exupéry, Antoine (1995 [1944]). *The Little Prince*. Ware: Wordsworth Editions.

DiCamillo, Kate (2006). *The Miraculous Journey of Edward Tulane*. Somerville, MA: Candlewick Press.

Dickens, Charles (1994 [1861]). *Great Expectations*. London: Penguin.

Dickinson, Emily (2016). *The Complete Poems*. London: Faber & Faber.

Dickinson, Emily (2018 [1860]). 'Dear March – Come In –', in Susannah Herbert (ed.), *Poetry for a Change*. Hereford: Otter-Barry Books.

Downing, Charles (1956). 'The Frost, the Sun, and the Wind', in *Russian Tales and Legends*. London: Oxford University Press.

Duffy, Carol Ann (ed.) (2012). *101 Poems for Children*. London: Macmillan.

Dunbar, Paul Laurence (1922). 'The Wind and the Sea', in *The Complete Poems of Paul Laurence Dunbar*. New York: Dodd, Mead & Company.

Dunbar, Paul Laurence (2014 [1899]). 'Sympathy', in *Lyrics of the Hearthside*. Miami, FL: HardPress Publishing.

Edge, Christopher (2016). *The Many Worlds of Albie Bright*. London: Nosy Crow.

Edge, Christopher (2019). *The Longest Night of Charlie Noon*. London: Nosy Crow.

Edwards, Amelia B. (2010 [1864]). 'The Phantom Coach', in Vic Parker (ed.), *Classic Ghost Stories*. Thaxted: Miles Kelly.

Fan, Eric and Fan, Terry (2016). *The Night Gardener*. New York: Simon & Schuster.

Farjeon, Eleanor (1958). 'Cat!', in *Silver, Sand and Snow*. London: Michael Joseph.

Fogliano, Julie (2018). *A House That Once Was*. London: Roaring Book Press.

Gaiman, Neil (2009). *The Graveyard Book*. London: Bloomsbury.

Gavin, Jamila (2014). 'Blackberry Blue', in *Blackberry Blue and Other Fairy Tales*. London: Random House.

Gleitzman, Morris (2005). *Once*. London: Puffin.

Gold, Hannah (2021). *The Last Bear*, ill. Levi Pinfold. London: HarperCollins.

Gold, Hannah (2022). *The Lost Whale*, ill. Levi Pinfold. London: HarperCollins.

Gross, Philip (2018). *Dark Sky Park: Poems from the Edge of Nature*, ill. Jesse Hodgson. Hereford: Otter-Barry Books.

Han-Shan (2013). *Cold Mountain Poems: Twenty-Four Poems by Han-Shan*, tr. Gary Snyder. Berkeley, CA: Counterpoint Press.

Hardy, Thomas (2015 [1917]). *Moments of Vision*. N.p.: CreateSpace.

Hardy-Dawson, Sue (2017). 'Fog Warning', in *Where Zebras Go*. Hereford: Otter-Barry Books.

Hardy-Dawson, Sue (2020). *If I Were Other Than Myself*. Ardleigh: Troika Books.

Ho-Yen, Polly (2015). *Boy in the Tower*. London: Random House.

Holub, Miroslav (1972). 'Fairy Tale', in Seamus Heaney and Ted Hughes (eds), *The Rattle Bag*. London: Faber & Faber.

Holub, Miroslav (2004 [1962]). 'The Door', in *Collected Later Poems 1988–2000*. Hexham: Bloodaxe Books.

Housman, Alfred E. (1994 [1896]). 'Blue Remembered Hills', in *The Collected Poems of A. E. Housman*. Ware: Wordsworth Editions.

Hughes, Langston (1995 [1926]). 'I, Too', in *The Collected Poems of Langston Hughes*. New York: Vintage Classics.

Hughes, Ted (1957). 'Wind', in *Hawk in the Rain*. London: Faber & Faber.

Hughes, Ted (1968). *The Iron Man*. London: Faber & Faber.

Hutchins, Pat (2009 [1974]). *When the Wind Blew*. New York: Simon & Schuster.

Janeczko, Paul B. (ed.) (2019). *The Proper Way to Meet a Hedgehog: And Other How-To Poems*, ill. Richard Jones. Somerville, MA: Candlewick Press.

Jeffers, Oliver (2017). *Here We Are: Notes for Living on Planet Earth*. London: HarperCollins.

Keats, John (1988 [1820]). 'To Autumn', in *John Keats: The Complete Poems*, 3rd edn. London: Penguin.

Koch, Kenneth (1990). *Rose, Where Did You Get That Red?* New York: Vintage Books.

Lewis, J. Patrick (2009). *The House*, ill. Roberto Innocenti. Mankato, MN: Creative Editions.

Litchfield, David (2017). *Grandad's Secret Giant*. London: Frances Lincoln.

López Merino, Francisco (1979 [*c.*1922]). 'Lonely Street', in Kate Webb (ed.), *I Like This Poem*. London: Puffin.

Lowell, Amy (2015 [1912]). 'A Coloured Print by Shokei', in *A Dome of Many-Coloured Glass*. N.p.: CreateSpace.

Magnason, Andri Snær (2013). *The Casket of Time*. New York: Restless Books.

Magorian, Michelle (1983). *Goodnight Mister Tom*. London: Puffin.

McAllister, Angela (2008). *Leon and the Place Between*, ill. Grahame Baker-Smith. Dorking: Templar Publishing.

McAnulty, Dara (2020). *Diary of a Young Naturalist*. Beaminster: Little Toller Books.

McAnulty, Dara (2021). *Wild Child: A Journey Through Nature*, ill. Barry Falls. London: Macmillan Children's Books.

McKay, Hilary (2017). 'Over the Hills and Far Away, or Red Riding Hood and the Piper's Son', in *Fairy Tales*. London: Macmillan.

McGough, Roger (2001). *100 Best Poems*. London: Penguin.

McGough, Roger (2003). 'Give and Take', in *All the Best: The Selected Poems of Roger McGough*. London: Puffin.

Mew, Charlotte (1997 [1929]). 'The Call', in Val Warner (ed.), *Charlotte Mew: Collected Poems and Selected Prose*. Manchester: Fyfield Books. (Now available as: *Charlotte Mew: Collected Poems and Selected Prose*. Abingdon and New York: Routledge, 2003.)

Millwood Hargrave, Kiran (2016). *The Girl of Ink and Stars*. Frome: Chicken House.

Millwood Hargrave, Kiran (2017). *The Island at the End of Everything*. Frome: Chicken House.

Millwood Hargrave, Kiran (2022). *Julia and the Shark*, ill. Tom de Freston. London: Orion.

Morpurgo, Michael (2009). *This Morning I Met a Whale*, ill. Christian Birmingham. London: Walker Books.

Morpurgo, Michael (2011 [1986]). *Why the Whales Came*. London: Egmont.

Morpurgo, Michael (2015). *I Believe in Unicorns*, ill. Gary Blythe. London: Walker Books.

Naidoo, Beverley (2000). *The Other Side of Truth*. London: Random House.

Naidoo, Beverley (2022). *Children of the Stone City*. London: HarperCollins.

Nesbit, Edith (1993 [1899]). 'The Island of the Nine Whirlpools', in Jan Mark (ed.), *Oxford Book of Children's Stories*. Oxford: Oxford University Press.

Nesbit, Edith (1999 [1902]). *Five Children and It*. Ware: Wordsworth Editions.

Nichols, Grace (1996). 'Hurricane Hits England', in *Sunris*. London: Virago.

Nova, Karl (2017). *Rhythm and Poetry*. Steeton: Caboodle Books.

Noyes, Alfred (2014 [1952]). 'The Highwayman', in *Collected Poems of Alfred Noyes, Volume 1*. London: Read Books.

Pullman, Philip (1995). *Northern Lights* (His Dark Materials). London: Scholastic.

Pullman, Philip (1996). *Clockwork*. London: Random House.

Reeves, James (2009 [1950]). 'Slowly', in *Complete Poems for Children*. London: Faber & Faber.

Reeves, James (2009 [1952]). 'A Garden at Night', in *Complete Poems for Children*. London: Faber & Faber.

Reeves, James (2009 [1957]). 'The Hippocrump', in *Complete Poems for Children*. London: Faber & Faber.

Rooney, Rachel (2021). 'The Language of Cat', in *The Language of Cat and Other Poems*. Hereford: Otter-Barry Books.

Rosen, Michael (2022). *What is a Bong Tree?* London: Michael Rosen Books.

Rossetti, Christina (2003 [1872]). 'Hurt No Living Thing', in *Sing-Song: A Nursery Rhyme Book*. New York: Dover Publications.

Rundell, Katherine (2015). *The Wolf Wilder*. London: Bloomsbury.

Said, S. F. (2022) *Tyger*, ill. Dave Mckean. Oxford: David Fickling Books.

Sánchez Vegara, Maria Isabel. (2020). *Little People, Big Dreams: Greta Thunberg*, ill. Anke Weckmann. London: Frances Lincoln.

Sandburg, Carl (1916). 'Fog', in *Poetry for Young People: Carl Sandburg*. New York: Stirling Books.

Seigal, Joshua (2022). *Yapping Away*, ill. Sarah Horne. London: Bloomsbury.

Sears, Rob and Sears, Tom (2021). *The Biggest Footprint: Eight Billion Humans. One Clumsy Giant*. Edinburgh: Canongate.

Shelley, Percy Bysshe (1994 [1818]). 'Ozymandias', in *The Selected Poetry and Prose of Shelley*. Ware: Wordsworth Editions.

Steen, David A. (2022). *Rewilding: Bringing Wildlife Back Where It Belongs*, ill. Chiara Fedele. New York: Neon Squid.

Stevenson, Robert Louis (1995 [1880]). *The Pavilion on the Links*. London: Penguin.

Stevenson, Robert Louis (2000 [1883]). *Treasure Island*. London: Penguin.

Stevenson, Robert Louis (2011 [1885]). 'The Little Land', in *A Child's Garden of Verses*. Glasgow: HarperCollins.

Stoker, Bram (1983 [1897]). *Dracula*. Oxford: Oxford University Press.

Tennyson, Alfred, Lord (1963 [1851]). 'The Eagle', in Edward Blishen (ed.), *Oxford Book of Poetry for Children*. London: Oxford University Press.

Tennyson, Alfred, Lord (1994a [1832]). 'The Lady of Shalott', in *The Works of Alfred Lord Tennyson*. Ware: Wordsworth Editions.

Tennyson, Alfred, Lord (1994b [1833]). 'Morte D'Arthur', in *The Works of Alfred Lord Tennyson*. Ware: Wordsworth Editions.

Tennyson, Alfred, Lord (2004 [1859]). *Idylls of the King*. New York: Dover Publications.

Thomas, Edward (1917). 'Adlestrop', in *The Works of Edward Thomas*. Ware: Wordsworth Editions.

Torday, Piers (2013). *The Last Wild*. London: Quercus Children's Books.

Tucker, Zoë (2019). *Greta and the Giants*, ill. Zoe Persico. London: Frances Lincoln.

Van den Ende, Peter (2019). *The Wanderer*. Amsterdam: Pushkin.

Verne, Jules (1996 [1864]). *Journey to the Centre of the Earth*. Ware: Wordsworth Editions.

Villa, Alvaro F. (2014). *Flood*. London: Curious Fox.

Wakeling, Kate (2016). *Moon Juice*. Birmingham: Emma Press.

Weil, Zaro (2019). *Cherry Moon: Little Poems Big Ideas Mindful of Nature*, ill. Junli Song. Ardleigh: Troika Books.

Weil, Zaro (2022). *When Poems Fall from the Sky*, ill. Junli Song. London: Welbeck Editions.

Wells, Herbert G. (2015 [1906]). 'The Door in the Wall', in *A Slip Under the Microscope*. London: Penguin.

Wiesner, David (1990). *Hurricane*. New York: Mifflin Harcourt.

Williams, Margery (2017 [1922]). *The Velveteen Rabbit*. London: Egmont.

Wolfe, Humbert (2012 [1925]). 'Green Candles', in Carol Ann Duffy (ed.), *101 Poems for Children: A Laureate's Choice*. London: Macmillan.

Wordsworth, William (1994 [1807]). 'I Wandered Lonely as a Cloud', in *The Collected Poems of William Wordsworth*. Ware: Wordsworth Editions.

Yeats, William Butler (2017 [1899]). 'The Song of Wandering Aengus', in *The Wind Among the Reeds*. London: Forgotten Books.

Yevtushenko, Yevgeny (2008 [1962]). 'The Companion', in *Yevtushenko: Selected Poems*, tr. Peter Levi and Robin Milner-Gulland. London: Penguin.

Secondary sources

Alexander, Robin (2020a). *A Dialogic Teaching Companion*. London and New York: Routledge.

Alexander, Robin (2020b). 'Dialogic Teaching Revisited: More Important Now Than Ever', *Chartered College* [webinar]. Available at: https://my.chartered.college/research-hub/webinar-dialogic-teaching-revisited-more-important-now-than-ever.

Ashley, Kelly (2019). *Word Power: Amplifying Vocabulary Instruction*. Norwich: Singular Publishing.

Bishop, Rudine S. (1990). 'Mirrors, Windows, and Sliding Glass Doors', *Perspectives: Choosing and Using Books for the Classroom*, 6(3): ix–xi.

Black, Paul, Harrison, Christine, Lee, Clare, Marshall, Bethan and Wiliam, Dylan (2002). *Working Inside the Black Box: Assessment for Learning in the Classroom*. London: GL Assessment.

Black, Paul and Wiliam, Dylan (1998). *Inside the Black Box: Raising Standards Through Classroom Assessment*. London: GL Assessment.

Blake, Julie V. (2019). What Did the National Curriculum Do for Poetry? Pattern, Prescription and Contestation in the Poetry Selected for GCSE English Literature 1988–2018. Unpublished dissertation, University of Cambridge. Available at: https://www.repository.cam. ac.uk/bitstream/handle/1810/300651/ Redacted-BLAKE-2019-PhD.pdf.

Bullock, Alan (1975). *A Language for Life* [Bullock Report]. London: Her Majesty's Stationery Office. Available at: http:// www.educationengland.org.uk/ documents/bullock/bullock1975.html.

Cain, Kate (2021). 'Reading for Meaning: The Importance of Oral Language Skills', *NATE Primary Matters* (spring): 4–8. Available at: https:// searchingforexcellence.co.uk/ wp-content/uploads/2021/03/ p4-8-reading-for-meaning.pdf.

Cervetti, Gina N., Wright, Tanya S. and Hwang, Hye-Jin (2016). 'Conceptual Coherence, Comprehension and Vocabulary Acquisition: A Knowledge Effect?', *Reading and Writing: An Interdisciplinary Journey*, 29(4): 761–779.

Chambers, Aidan (2011 [1993]). *Tell Me: Children, Reading and Talk* and *The Reading Environment: How Adults Help Children Enjoy Books*. Stroud: Thimble Press.

Clandfield, Lindsay (2002). 'Writing Skills: Mini Saga', *Onestopenglish*. Available at: https://www.onestopenglish.com/ writing/writing-skills-mini-saga/146335. article.

Clarke, Shirley (2014). *Outstanding Formative Assessment: Culture and Practice*. London: Hodder & Stoughton.

Clarke, Shirley (2021). *Formative Assessment: A Little Guide for Teachers*. London: SAGE.

Clements, James (2018). *Teaching English by the Book: Putting Literature at the Heart of the Primary Curriculum*. Abingdon and New York: Routledge.

Clements, James (2023). *On the Write Track: A Practical Guide to Teaching Writing in Primary Schools*. Abingdon and New York: Routledge.

Clements, James and Tobin, Mathew (2021). *Understanding and Teaching Primary English: Theory into Practice*. London: SAGE.

Coe, Robert, Aloisi, Cesare, Higgins, Steve and Elliot Major, Lee (2014). *What Makes Great Teaching? Review of the Underpinning Research*. London: Sutton Trust. Available at: https://www. suttontrust.com/our-research/ great-teaching.

Corbett, Pie and Strong, Julia (2019). *Talk for Writing Across the Curriculum: How to Teach Non-Fiction Writing to 5–12-Year-Olds*, 2nd edn. London: David Fulton.

Cordingley, Philippa and Bell, Miranda (2007). *Transferring Learning and Taking Innovation to Scale*. Penrith: CUREE. Available at: http://www.curee.co.uk/ files/publication/1236960866/ Transferring%20learning%20and%20 taking%20innovation%20to%20 scale%20-%20think%20piece.pdf.

Cordingley, Philippa, Higgins, Steve, Greany, Toby, Buckler, Natalia, Coles-Jordan, Deanna, Crisp, Bart, Saunders, Lesley and Coe, Robert (2015). *Developing Great Teaching: Lessons from the International Reviews into Effective Professional Development*. London: Teacher Development Trust. Available at: https:// tdtrust.org/about/dgt.

Cox, Bob (2021). 'Rich Knowledge, Deep Response', *Teach Reading & Writing*, 13: 70–71. Available at: https://ace-mags. s3.eu-west-2.amazonaws.com/trw/ TRW-2021/6/index.html.

Davie, Ronald, Butler, Neville R. and Goldstein, Harvey (1972). *From Birth to Seven: A Report of the National Child Development Study*. London: Longman, in association with the National Children's Bureau.

Department for Education (2013). *English Programmes of Study – Key Stages 1 and 2: National Curriculum in England* (September; rev. 16 July 2014). Available at: https://www.gov.uk/government/uploads/system/uploads/attachment_data/file/335186/PRIMARY_national_curriculum_-_English_220714.pdf.

Department for Education (2014). National Curriculum in England: English Programmes of Study (16 July). Available at: https://www.gov.uk/government/publications/national-curriculum-in-england-english-programmes-of-study.

Department for Education (2020). *Development Matters: Non-Statutory Curriculum Guidance for the Early Years Foundation Stage* (rev. July 2021). Available at: https://www.gov.uk/government/publications/development-matters--2.

Department for Education (2021). *The Reading Framework: Teaching the Foundations of Literacy.* Available at: https://www.gov.uk/government/publications/the-reading-framework-teaching-the-foundations-of-literacy.

Department for Education and Employment (2001). *Key Stage 3 National Strategy: English Department Training.* London: DfEE.

Department for Education and Skills (1998). *The National Literacy Strategy: Framework for Teaching*, 3rd edn. Nottingham: DfES. Available at: https://dera.ioe.ac.uk//4699.

Department for Education and Skills (2006). *Primary National Strategy: Primary Framework for Literacy and Mathematics.* Nottingham: DfES. Available at: http://www.educationengland.org.uk/documents/pdfs/2006-primary-national-strategy.pdf.

Department of Education Western Australia (2013). *Reading Resource Book: Addressing Current Literacy Challenges.* Available at: https://myresources.education.wa.edu.au/docs/default-source/resources/first-steps-literacy/first002.pdf.

Doherty, Jonathan (2021). 'Levelling the Playing Field and Promoting Social Mobility through Education' in *Future of Teaching: Celebrating Teacher Expertise.*

London: Chartered College of Teaching, pp. 22–29. Available at: https://chartered.college/future-of-teaching.

Duke, Nell K. and Pearson, P. David (2002). 'Effective Practices for Developing Reading Comprehension'. In Alan Farstrup and Jay Samuels (eds), *What Research Has to Say About Reading Instruction.* Newark, DE: International Reading Association, pp. 205–242.

Durran, James (2021). 'Key Learning Questions: An Introduction' (28 August). Available at: https://jamesdurran.blog/2021/08/28/key-learning-questions-an-introduction.

Eaglestone, Robert (2017). *Doing English: A Guide for Literature Students*, 4th edn. Abingdon and New York: Routledge.

Eaglestone, Robert (2019). *Literature: Why It Matters.* Cambridge: Polity Press.

Eaglestone, Robert (2021). ' "Powerful Knowledge", "Cultural Literacy" and the Study of Literature in Schools', *Impact*, 26. Available at: https://onlinelibrary.wiley.com/doi/full/10.1111/2048-416X.2020.12006.x.

Education Policy Institute (2017). *Closing the Gap? Trends in Educational Attainment and Disadvantage.* London: Education Policy Institute.

Eyre, Deborah (2011). *Room at the Top: Inclusive Education for High Performance.* London: Policy Exchange. Available at: https://www.policyexchange.org.uk/wp-content/uploads/2016/09/room-at-the-top-apr-11-2.pdf.

Eyre, Deborah (2016). *High Performance Learning: How to Become a World Class School.* Abingdon and New York: Routledge.

Farquharson, Christine, McNally, Sandra and Tahir, Imran (2022a). 'Education Inequalities' [IFS Deaton Review of Inequalities]. London: Institute for Fiscal Studies. Available at: https://ifs.org.uk/inequality/wp-content/uploads/2022/08/Education-inequalities.pdf.

Farquharson, Christine, McNally, Sandra and Tahir, Imran (2022b). 'Lack of Progress on Closing Educational Inequalities Disadvantaging Millions Throughout Life', *Institute for Fiscal Studies* [press release] (16 August). Available at:

https://ifs.org.uk/news/lack-progress-closing-educational-inequalities-disadvantaging-millions-throughout-life.

Ferguson, Felicity (2021). 'Are You for Real?', *Teach Reading & Writing*, issue 12, 44–45. Available at: https://writing4pleasure.com/wp-content/uploads/2021/05/trw-2021-pages-48-49.pdf.

Gadsby, Ben (2017). *Impossible? Social Mobility and the Seemingly Unbreakable Class Ceiling*. London: Teach First.

Gamble, Nikki (2019). *Exploring Children's Literature: Reading for Knowledge, Understanding and Pleasure*, 4th edn. London: SAGE.

Gaunt, Amy and Stott, Alice (2019). *Transforming Teaching and Learning Through Talk: The Oracy Imperative*. London: Rowman & Littlefield.

Gilbert, Lisa, Terevainen, Anne, Clark, Christina and Shaw, Sophia (2018). *Literacy and Life Expectancy: An Evidence Review Exploring the Link Between Literacy and Life Expectancy in England Through Health and Socioeconomic Factors*. London: National Literacy Trust. Available at: https://literacytrust.org.uk/research-services/research-reports/literacy-and-life-expectancy.

Haig, Joan and Lennon, Joan (2022). *Talking History: 150 Years of Speakers and Speeches*, ill. André Ducci. London: Templar Publishing.

Helman, Zoe and Gibbs, Sam (2022). *The Trouble with English and How to Address It: A Practical Guide to Delivering a Concept-Led Curriculum*. Abingdon and New York: Routledge.

Hochman, Judith C. and Wexler, Natalie (2017). *The Writing Revolution: A Guide to Advancing Thinking Through Writing in All Subjects and Grades*. San Francisco, CA: Jossey-Bass.

Hope, Kerry (2021). 'Spotlight on Ryefield Primary School', *NATE Primary Matters* (autumn): 55–58. Available at: https://searchingforexcellence.co.uk/wp-content/uploads/2021/11/ryefield-school-journey.pdf.

Horton, Suzanne, Beattie, Louise and Lannie, Sharon (2019). *Reading at Greater Depth in Key Stage 2* (Exploring the Primary Curriculum). London: SAGE.

Hughes, Ted (1967). *Poetry in the Making: A Handbook for Writing and Teaching*. London: Faber & Faber.

Kaiser, Niki (2020). 'Meaningful Memory', *Norwich Research School* (3 September). Available at: https://researchschool.org.uk/norwich/news/meaningful-memory.

Lemov, Doug, Driggs, Colleen and Woolway, Erica (2016). *Reading Reconsidered: A Practical Guide to Rigorous Literacy Instruction*. San Francisco, CA: Jossey-Bass.

Mansworth, Megan (2021). *Teach to the Top: Aiming High for Every Learner*. Woodbridge: John Catt Educational.

Meek, Margaret (1988). *How Texts Teach What Readers Learn*. Stroud: Thimble Press.

Meek Spencer, Margaret (2001). 'Preface', in Myra Barrs and Valerie Cork, *The Reader in the Writer: The Links Between the Study of Literature and Writing Development at Key Stage 2*. London: Centre for Language in Primary Education, pp. 9–20.

Miliband, David (2004). 'Personalised Learning: Building a New Relationship with Schools'. Speech delivered at the North of England Education Conference, Belfast, 8 January.

Miller, Donalyn (2009). *The Book Whisperer*. San Francisco, CA: Jossey-Bass.

Morpurgo, Michael (2016). 'The Power of Stories'. Book Trust lecture, London, 21 September. Available at: https://www.michaelmorpurgo.com/michael-morpurgo-book-trust-lecture.

Myatt, Mary (2018). *The Curriculum: Gallimaufry to Coherence*. Woodbridge: John Catt Educational.

Myatt, Mary (2020a). *Back on Track: Fewer Things, Greater Depth*. Woodbridge: John Catt Educational.

Myatt, Mary (2020b). 'Death By Differentiation' (19 December). Available at: https://www.marymyatt.com/blog/death-by-differentiation.

Myhill, Debra, Jones, Susan, Lines, Helen and Watson, Annabel (2012). 'Re-thinking Grammar: The Impact of Embedded Grammar Teaching on Students' Writing and Students' Metalinguistic Understanding', *Research Papers in Education*, 27(2): 139–166.

Myhill, Debra, Jones, Susan, Watson, Annabel and Lines, Helen (2016). *Essential Primary Grammar*. Maidenhead: Open University Press.

National Association for Able Children in Education (2020). *Making Space for Able Learners. Cognitive Challenge: Principles into Practice*. Didcot: NACE.

Newbolt, Henry (1921). *The Teaching of English in England: Being the Report of the Departmental Committee Appointed by the President of the Board of Education to Inquire into the Position of English in the Educational System of England* [Newbolt Report]. London: His Majesty's Stationery Office. Available at: http://www.educationengland.org.uk/documents/newbolt/newbolt1921.html.

Nuthall, Graham (2007). *The Hidden Lives of Learners*. Wellington: New Zealand Council for Educational Research.

Nystrand, Martin with Gamoran, Adam, Kachur, Robert and Prendergast, Catherine (1997). *Opening Dialogue: Understanding the Dynamics of Language and Learning in the English Classroom*. New York: Teachers College Press.

Oakhill, Jane, Cain, Kate and Elbro, Carsten (2014). *Understanding and Teaching Reading Comprehension: A Handbook*. Abingdon and New York: Routledge.

Robertson, Dawn (2020). 'You Can Never Have Too Much Poetry', *NATE Primary Matters* (autumn): 14–18. Available at: https://www.nate.org.uk/wp-content/uploads/2020/09/Primary-Matters-10-Autumn-2020.pdf.

Rosen, Michael (2016). *What is Poetry? The Essential Guide to Reading and Writing Poems*. London: Walker Books.

Rosen, Michael (2018). *Why Write? Why Read?* Milton Keynes: Lightning Source.

Rosenblatt, Louise (1978). *The Reader, the Text, the Poem: The Transactional Theory of the Literary Work*. Carbondale, IL: Southern Illinois Press.

Shanahan, Timothy (2018). 'Where Questioning Fits in Comprehension Instruction: Skills and Strategies Part II', *Shanahan on Literacy* (28 May). Available at: https://www.shanahanonliteracy.com/blog/where-questioning-fits-in-comprehension-instruction-skills-and-strategies-part-ii.

Standards and Testing Agency (2018). *Teacher Assessment Frameworks at the End of Key Stage 2*. Available at: https://www.gov.uk/government/publications/teacher-assessment-frameworks-at-the-end-of-key-stage-2.

Steel, Abigail (2021). *Rocket Phonics Teacher Guide 1* (Rising Stars Reading Planet). London: Hodder & Stoughton.

Such, Christopher (2021). *The Art and Science of Teaching Primary Reading*. London: Corwin.

Tennent, Wayne (2015). *Understanding Reading Comprehension: Processes and Practices*. London: SAGE.

Thompson, Sonia (2022). *Berger's An Ethic of Excellence in Action*. Woodbridge: John Catt Educational.

Thunberg, Greta (2019). 'Our House Is On Fire'. Address at the World Economic Forum, Davos, 25 January. Available at: https://awpc.cattcenter.iastate.edu/2019/12/02/address-at-davos-our-house-is-on-fire-jan-25-2019.

Warwick, Ian and Speakman, Ray (2019). *Learning with Leonardo: Unfinished Perfection*. Woodbridge: John Catt Educational.

Westbrook, Jo, Sutherland, Julia, Oakhill, Jane and Sullivan, Susan (2019). '"Just Reading": The Impact of a Faster Pace of Reading Narratives on the Comprehension of Poorer Adolescent Readers in English Classrooms', *Literacy*, 53(2): 60–68. Available at: http://sro.sussex.ac.uk/id/eprint/70702.

Wexler, Natalie (2019). *The Knowledge Gap: The Hidden Cause of America's Broken Education System – And How to Fix It*. New York: Avery.

Wexler, Natalie (2022a). '7 Ways Our Intuition Can Mislead Us About Learning', *Forbes* (3 January). Available at: https://www.forbes.com/sites/

nataliewexler/2022/01/03/7-ways-our-intuition-can-mislead-us-about-learning/?sh=422a044112f1.

Wexler, Natalie (2022b). ' "What Works" in Reading Comprehension – And What Doesn't', *Forbes* (9 April). Available at: https://www.forbes.com/sites/nataliewexler/2022/04/09/what-works-in-reading-comprehension-and-what-doesnt.

Yates, Denise (2022). *Parenting Dual Exceptional Children: Supporting a Child who Has High Learning Potential and Special Educational Needs and Disabilities*. London: Jessica Kingsley.

Young, Ross and Ferguson, Felicity (2021). *Writing for Pleasure: Theory, Research and Practice*. Abingdon and New York: Routledge.

Online resources

Book Trust: https://www.booktrust.org.uk

British Library: https://www.bl.uk/childrens-books/themes/non-fiction

Centre for Literacy and Social Justice: https://wels.open.ac.uk/research/lsj

Centre for Literacy in Primary Education (CLPE): https://clpe.org.uk

Federation of Children's Book Groups: https://fcbg.org.uk

HFL Education: https://www.hertsforlearning.co.uk

High Performance Learning: https://highperformancelearning.co.uk

Let's Think in English: https://www.letsthinkinenglish.org

National Association for the Teaching of English: https://www.nate.org.uk

Open University: https://ourfp.org

Oracy Cambridge: https://oracycambridge.org

Potential Plus UK: https://potentialplusuk.org

Potential Trust: https://www.thepotentialtrust.org.uk

Searching for Excellence: https://searchingforexcellence.co.uk/poetry-resources

Talk for Writing (Pie Corbett): https://shop.talk4writing.com and https://www.talk4writing.com/talk-for-reading

United Kingdom Literacy Association (UKLA): https://ukla.org

University of Exeter (Writing Resources for Teachers): https://education.exeter.ac.uk/research/centres/writing/grammar-teacher-resources

List of online resources

All the key texts referenced and illustrations to support your work in the classroom can be downloaded at: www.crownhouse.co.uk/ opening-doors-ambitious-primary-english.

Resource 1   Pitching High and Including All illustration (p. 6).

Resource 2   Challenge and response illustration (p. 16).

Resource 3   Extract from *Tamarind and the Star of Ishta by* Jasbinder Bilan (p. 19).

Resource 4   Text Choice and Concepts illustration (p. 30).

Resource 5   Extract from *Treasure Island* by Robert Louis Stevenson (p. 34).

Resource 6   Quality Text to Quality Writing illustration (p. 42).

Resource 7   Extract from 'Fog Warning', from *Where Zebras Go* by Sue Hardy-Dawson (p. 45).

Resource 8   Principles to Strategies illustration (p. 54).

Resource 9   Extract from 'Ozymandias' by Percy Bysshe Shelley (pp. 57-58).

Resource 10   Link Reading illustration (p. 66).

Resource 11   Extract from 'The Wind and the Sea' by Paul Laurence Dunbar's (p. 71).

Resource 12   Taster Drafts: Writing for Reading illustration (p. 78).

Resource 13   Extract from *October, October* by Katya Balen (p. 81).

Resource 14   Learning Dialogues illustration (p. 92).

Resource 15   Excellence Success Criteria illustration (p. 106).

Resource 16   Extract from *Where the River Runs Gold* © Sita Brahmachari (pp. 107–108).

Resource 17   Radial Question Layouts illustration (p. 118).

About the Authors

Bob Cox

Bob Cox is the award-winning author of the 'Opening Doors' series and a long-term educationist, writer, teacher and consultant. He has presented at regional, national and international conferences exploring principles and strategies for exciting, ambitious English. He is constantly emphasising the critical role of the teacher in taking pupils to new levels of thinking and reading – the routes to equity and excellence. Literature, libraries and schools change lives. @BobCox_SFE

Julie Sargent

Julie Sargent has over ten years' experience of working across the whole of the primary sector as an English consultant. This includes developing bespoke CPD for individual schools, multi-academy trusts and local authorities. She has a particular interest in the early years/Key Stage 1 and using high-quality texts to promote and develop all aspects of English. @Julie_Sargent1

Leah Crawford

Leah Crawford has fifteen years' experience as a local authority English inspector and adviser, working across both primary and secondary phases, and now leads ThinkTalk education consultancy. She is a tutor for King's College London's Let's Think in English cognitive acceleration programme and has supported a European Erasmus project on the assessment of thinking skills. Her master's in education focused on professional development for the teaching of thinking through dialogue. @think_talk_org

Angela Jenkins

Angela Jenkins has extensive experience in English education and school improvement having worked as an adviser in three different local authorities and two multi-academy trusts in the last twenty years. As well as providing link adviser support for individual schools, she also took strategic responsibility for English and assessment. Recently, Angela has worked as an independent consultant, providing specialist advice and support for the development of exceptional curriculum, pedagogy and assessment in both primary and secondary settings. She is currently co-chair of the National Association of Advisers in English. @MuchAdoALJ

Victoria Cox

Since childhood, Vicky has always loved reading and expressing herself through painting and drawing. Now based in Brighton with her own family, working with her dad to bring these texts to life through her illustrations has been a dream project.

Opening Doors to a Richer English Curriculum
for Ages 6 to 9
Bob Cox with Leah Crawford and Verity Jones
ISBN: 978-178583398-4

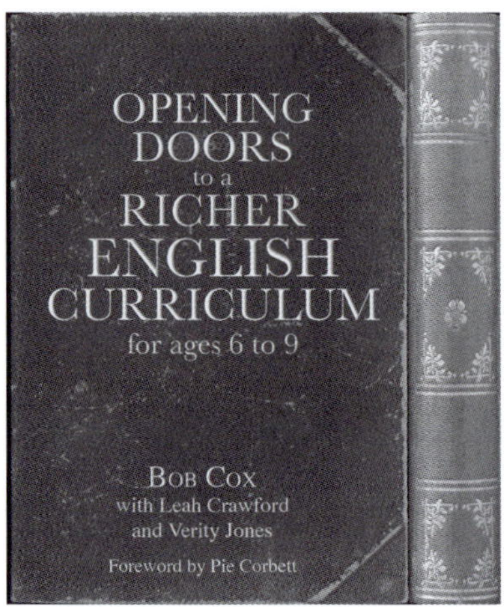

Opening Doors to a Richer English Curriculum
for Ages 10 to 13
Bob Cox with Leah Crawford and Verity Jones
ISBN: 978-178583397-7

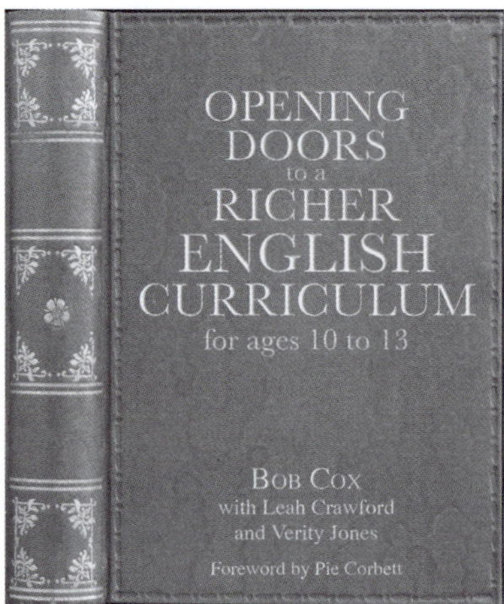

Opening Doors to Quality Writing
Ideas for writing inspired by great writers for ages 6 to 9
Bob Cox
ISBN: 978-178583013-6

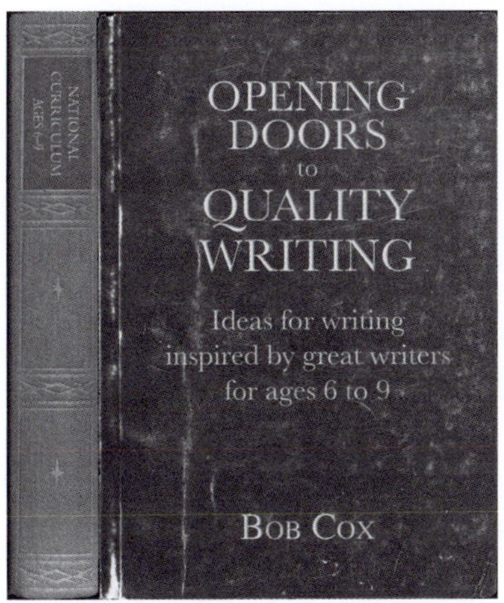

Opening Doors to Quality Writing
Ideas for writing inspired by great writers for ages 10 to 13
Bob Cox
ISBN: 978-178583014-3

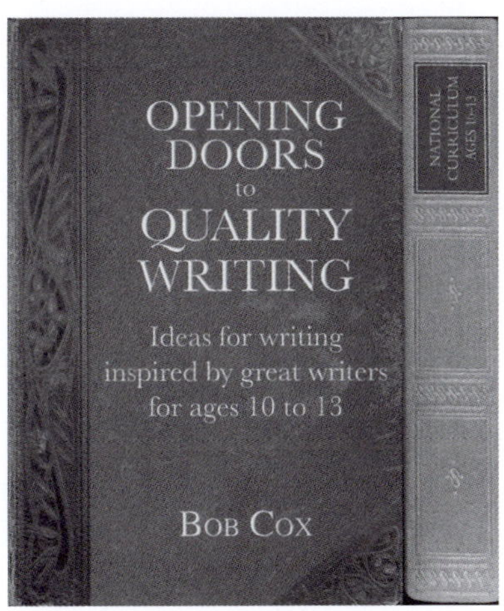

Opening Doors to Famous Poetry and Prose

Ideas and resources for accessing literary heritage works

Bob Cox

ISBN: 978-184590896-6

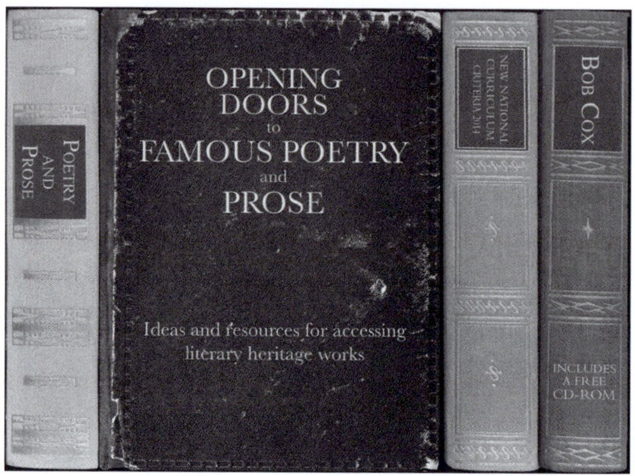

Opening Doors to Famous Poetry and Prose provides 20 units of work covering poetry and prose from our literary heritage. Each unit comes with exciting stimulus material and creative suggestions for ways in which the material can be used for outstanding learning possibilities. Illustrations and innovative ideas to help pupils access the meaning and wonder of the text add to the book's appeal.

Pupils are encouraged, throughout the units of work, to engage with language, invent questions and write with flair and accuracy, bringing literature from the past to life and opening doors to further reading and exploration.

Also included is an introduction to the concepts used in the book and suggestions for a range of methods and pathways which can lead to language development and literary appreciation. Although the units are diverse and have a range of poetry and prose for teachers to use, the book presents cohesive methods for engaging children with a variety of different literary texts and improving standards of literacy.

For teachers of pupils aged 7 to 13.